Game On!

OTHER REDLEAF PRESS BOOKS BY LINDA ARMSTRONG

Family Child Care Homes: Creative Spaces for Children to Learn
Great Afterschool Programs and Spaces That Wow!

Game On!

Screen-Free Fun for Children Two and Up

Linda J. Armstrong

Redleaf Press®
www.redleafpress.org
800-423-8309

Published by Redleaf Press
10 Yorkton Court
St. Paul, MN 55117
www.redleafpress.org

First edition 2018
Cover design by Jim Handrigan
Cover photographs © iStock.com/BraunS
Interior design by Heidi Hogg and Jim Handrigan
Typeset in Abril Text
Printed in the United States of America
25 24 23 22 21 20 19 18   1 2 3 4 5 6 7 8

Library of Congress Cataloging-in-Publication Data
CIP data for this book is available from the Library of Congress

Printed on acid-free paper

DEDICATION

This book is dedicated to everyone who enjoys playing a game as much as winning it. I have lost far more times than I have won but still continue to play. Grantland Rice famously wrote "It is not whether you win or lose; it's about how you play the game." This quote reminds me to enjoy the game as much as the outcome, be a gracious winner or loser, and always keep my game face on.

So here's to all of you who feel life is a game that we learn early on and keep playing when we get old. It's only when we quit that we lose.

"Life is more fun if you play games" —Roald Dahl

CONTENTS

PREFACE

Life is a game, play it.
—Mother Teresa

I learned the value of games on a hot day many years ago while waiting in line with my family to tour the Washington Monument. The line never seemed to move, and our kids' patience was nonexistent. "Let's play a game," I said. "Whoever guesses the time closest to when we get to the front of the line and into the elevator gets to choose where we'll eat dinner tonight." Let the game begin! Our two daughters, who love games, decided this was a great idea, and much to my surprise, so did others waiting with us. Each player chose the time they would walk into the monument with the park ranger. A timekeeper was assigned to keep track of all players' guesses. When a time passed that someone had guessed incorrectly, we all clapped and gave them high fives. Even the park ranger got into the game and offered to let the winner assist him with his elevator duties. This game kept our family as well as many others around us entertained, actually enjoying waiting in line, and it created a wonderful family memory too.

Games are played by young and old all around the world. Some games are played by ourselves while others are played with a group. In some respects, it just seems we are born to play. Babies love Peeka-boo and This Little Piggy, while adults often enjoy more sophisticated games like mah-jongg and bridge. All games have their own rules, but what they have in common is why we play . . . because games are engaging and entertaining.

In today's world, we see more and more games played on a screen rather than with someone or with something real to touch. Electronic games are exciting for the person playing, no doubt, but are we able to make memories in front of a screen the same as way as when interacting with others? Results of a recent survey of adults found their average screen time is nearly eight hours a day. In 2011 Common Sense Media issued a report called *Zero to Eight: Children's*

Media Use in America. This study found that children ages six months to six years old spend, on average, two hours per day on screened devices. The American Academy of Pediatrics has issued numerous reports about how the amount of time children spend in front of equipment with screens affects their development, attention span, behavior, and even rates of obesity.

Electronic games for children of all ages are easy to access and use. Screened devices have a kaleidoscope of colors. Quick animations and lively music have hypnotic effects on players. Nevertheless, there comes a time each day when everyone needs to have literal face time, not screen time. This book provides face-to-face gaming experiences for all ages.

Game On! is full of screen-free, traditional games and activities for young players who require nothing more than people, simple materials, and their brains to play. Minimal planning time is needed, and all games are easily adaptable according to players' ages, interests, or abilities. All children can play these games. So too can parents, grandparents, and teachers, really anyone and anywhere. I've written this book and divided games into sections so you can choose a game that fits the age and abilities of players, the amount of game time or space available, or the energy level needed.

My hope is for this book to be a practical resource for adults who remember the fun of playing games in their own childhood and who want to guide children today so they too will have great memories of playing games with friends and family.

Game on!

CHAPTER 1

RULES TO PLAY BY

We must be consistent in all games by having a set of rules that guides players in how they will play. Every game in this book has its own set of rules that includes how many players, how to score points, or even when or where to play the game. Rules need to be clear and understood by all players before the game begins. Also, they should be flexible enough to help players of all ages and abilities be successful. Rules that downplay competition and play up cooperation promote a winning feeling in all players.

It may take some players longer to become active participants in a game. Often, young children enjoy being spectators before they become players. One way to encourage participation is to allow players to create a rule or two to help them feel included in a game.

The list here includes some general guidelines when it comes to playing games as well as a few rules about being a good sport:

- Play by the rules of a game all of the time (even when no one sees you) to make sure the game is fair, fun, and safe.
- Be polite: wait your turn, compliment other players on their efforts or success, say "thank you," help another player who needs help, and say something that encourages others.
- Try your best and remember that other players are too.
- Include everyone who wants to play the game.
- Be a good winner: don't brag, show off, or put other players down while you're celebrating. Shake hands at the end of the game.
- Be a good loser: don't blame others or the rules, learn from your mistakes, remember that you can't win every time.

Simple Rules to Play By

This book has a section devoted to games appropriate for toddlers, up to age three on page xx. Rules for toddlers must be kept simple so they can understand. Four simple rules help toddlers learn how to play games:

1. Take turns.
2. Share.
3. Help each other.
4. Use kind words.

> *Taking turns* means everyone has the opportunity to be an active participant one at a time, such as "you go, then I go, then she goes," while *sharing* can mean having the same access to materials and time, such as passing them around without one player dominating or disallowing others from playing.

"Just for Fun" Rules

Make up wild and wacky rules not just for a game but also for a period of time spanning many activities, locations, and players, such as "rules only for today," "stay-inside day rules," or "rules while visiting a friend or relative." These are not only fun but also engaging. The following is a list of suggested "just for fun" rules:

- Hop over any door threshold whenever entering or leaving a room.
- Clap your hands every time someone says your name.
- Say, "Hi, there!" every time you see yourself in the mirror.
- Put your hands on your head anytime you hear a certain sound, such as a dog bark, car horn, or telephone ring.
- Skip instead of walk from place to place.

CHAPTER 2

WHO'S IT?

One of the most difficult parts of any game is figuring out who goes first, who will be It, or who will be the dealer, the leader, or have a starring role in a game. Not all players want this role and may choose to not enter into the selection process. What is important is that all players can decide for themselves what their role in a game will be. Here are a few ways to determine who starts the game as the leader or It.

> The player who wins the minigame gets to go first, be It, or be the dealer or the leader.

Games to Start Games

- One player flips a coin and hides it with one hand after it lands. The other player calls either heads or tails. If she guessed correctly, she wins. If she guessed incorrectly, the player who flipped the coin wins.
- One player puts a coin in one hand behind her back. The other player guesses which hand has the coin. If the player guesses correctly, he wins; if he guesses incorrectly, the player holding the coin wins.
- One player holds a group of sticks in a closed fist. Players guess how many sticks there are. The correct or closest answer to the actual number wins.

- One player holds one straw or stick for each player in her hand. One straw or stick should be shorter than the rest. The player holding the sticks uses her hand to cover the bottom of the sticks so that other players cannot see the length. Each player draws a stick. The player that draws the shortest stick wins.

- Each player rolls a die. Highest roll wins.

- A box of toothpicks is emptied onto a table. Each player picks up toothpicks one at a time, taking turns. The player who picks up the last toothpick wins.

- Each player takes turns putting one hand at a time on a stick, bat, or handle of a racket. Players place their hand above the player before them. The player to place his hand on the top wins.

- One player thinks of a number from one to ten. Other players guess the number until someone guesses correctly. The correct number wins.

- Play Rock, Paper, Scissors. Two players sit or stand face to face. In unison, players tap one fist in the palm on their other hand two times and on the third time, show their chosen motion, either rock (a fist), paper (a flat hand), or scissors (the pointer and middle fingers are extended in a V configuration). Winning hands are any of the following: Rock breaks scissors. Scissors cuts paper. Paper covers rock. A point is given to the player with a winning hand. If both players have identical motions, no points are awarded. The first player to get to a predetermined number of points is the winner.

Rhymes to Start Games

- All players except for one stand in a straight line. The player not in the line covers her eyes and points to the other players, one at a time, while chanting:

Blue shoe, blue shoe, how old are you?

The player pointed to at the end of the chant tells her age. Starting with the player who gave her age, the chanter counts shoes, two per player, out loud up to the number of the age given. The player touched last wins.

- All players except for one stand in a circle with their hands curled into a fist. Players hold both of their fists out into the middle of the circle. One player walks around the inside of the circle and touches each player's fists, one at a time, including their own, while chanting:

One potato, two potato, three potato, four.

Five potato, six potato, seven potato, more.

The player whose fist is touched on the word "more," puts that hand behind her, and the chant begins again until there is only one player left with a fist in the circle. The last player with a fist in the circle wins.

- All players stand in a circle facing each other. One player points to others one at a time, including themselves, while chanting:

Icka bicka soda cracker

Icka bicka boo;

Icka bicka soda cracker,

I pick Y-O-U.

The player touched on the letter "u" wins.

- All players stand in a circle putting one foot in the middle so it touches the other player's feet. One player begins tapping each foot in the circle, one at a time, while chanting:

Bub-ble-gum bub-ble-gum in a dish,

How man-y piec-es do you wish?

The player whose foot is touched on the word "wish" chooses a number. The player tapping feet continues tapping each foot up to the number chosen. The player whose foot is touched on the last number wins.

- All players except one stand in a straight line. The player not in line touches each player on the shoulder while chanting:

One, two, sky blue,

All are out except for you.

The player touched on the word "you" wins.

> **Note:** This rhyme is most appropriate for a small group of players.

- One player says, "one, two, three, not It!" All other players say "not It" as quickly as possible after the count of three. The last player to say "not it" will be It.
- All players except for one stand in a circle with their hands curled into a fist. Players hold both of their fists out into the middle of the circle. One player walks around the inside of the circle and touches each player's fists, one at a time, including their own, while chanting:

Mr. Mouse built a house,

How many bricks did he use?

The player whose fist is touched on the word "use" chooses a number. Then the player not in the circle continues to tap fists up to the number chosen. The player whose fist is touched on the final number wins.

CHAPTER 3

GAMES FROM AROUND THE WORLD

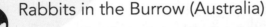

 ### Rabbits in the Burrow (Australia)

This game needs a minimum of ten players. Players form a circle and count off. Without touching any of the other players, two players hold hands to form a small circle, called the burrow. Player three is a rabbit and stands inside the burrow. Player four is the dingo, an Australian wild dog. All other players except player five are rabbits, outside of the burrow. The rabbits' job is to stay as far away from the dingo as possible while staying within the designated playing area. When all players are in place, player five gives the "Go" signal, and the dingo chases rabbits not in the burrow. If the dingo gets too close, a rabbit can run into the burrow, and the rabbit in the burrow must leave. One rabbit must be in the burrow at all times. This continues until the dingo catches a rabbit. Then the caught rabbit becomes the new dingo. Players can regroup and count off again for new roles in additional rounds of play.

Fisherman (Ghana)

This game needs at least six players. One player makes a large irregular shape on the ground, using chalk or tape, to draw a lake. Two to four players become fishermen and are given a long piece of rope, which is their fishing net. One player is the leader, and at her "Go" signal, the other players (fish) walk and move their arms as if swimming around in the lake while singing any well-known song. The fishermen work together, holding on to the rope, and wade into the lake. Then the fisherman can move only in a forward motion. If a fisherman touches a fish with any part of the rope, the fish is out and moves outside the lake until the next round.

Fish try to swim behind the net to avoid getting caught. When all fish are caught, a new game starts with new fishermen.

Cat and Mice (Philippines)

This game is played by a minimum of six players. One player is the cat. The other players, the mice, stand in a semicircle in front of the seated cat. Objects such as small rocks, sticks, balls, leaves, or flowers called "treasures" are laid in front of the cat. The cat's job is to guard the treasures while the mice try to divert the cat's attention and steal one or more treasures. To stop the mice, the cat must tag them. If a mouse is tagged, the cat retrieves the treasure. When all the treasures have been stolen, the game starts again with a new cat.

Stop! (Mexico)

Stop! needs only two players, each with a sheet of paper and a pen or pencil. Players draw vertical lines on their paper to divide it into six columns, and they work together to choose five categories to write at the top of each of the first five columns, such as animals, flowers, colors, or favorite foods. The last column is left blank for keeping score. One player starts the game by reciting the alphabet out loud until the next player says to stop. When the player stops on a letter, all other players write words starting with that letter in all five of their categories while the first player counts slowly to fifty. When time is up, players take turns reading aloud the words they have in each category. Players get a point for each word that starts with the correct letter in each category. After points have been calculated, players put their score in the last column. The player with the highest score starts the next round of play by reciting the alphabet out loud. After all players have had a turn to choose the letter (or one player reaches a predetermined number of points), the game is over. The player with the highest overall score is the winner.

Statues (Greece)

This game needs at least six players and is based on the poses of famous Greek statues. One player is It and stands in the center of an open playing area with his eyes covered. He starts counting slowly. Meanwhile, the other players scatter and run around the playing area. Although It must count at least to ten, there is no predetermined ending number. At some point, he stops counting, opens his eyes, and shouts "*Agalmata!*" (That means "statue" in Greek.) Then all other players must immediately freeze while trying to look like a famous statue they have seen, such as Paul Revere on his horse, Abraham Lincoln sitting on his chair, the Statue of Liberty, or others. Players can use props, such as sticks, a ball, or a chair, to look more authentic. After players strike a pose, they must hold it as long as they can. The player who is It tries to make the statues laugh or move without touching them. If a statue does move, she must run from the player who is It. Then the player who is It tries to tag her, and if he is successful, she is out of that round of play. The last player remaining statuesque is the winner and becomes the new It.

> Variation: One player is the sculptor and the others, the statues. The sculptor spins a player slowly and gently one or two times saying what she is sculpting the player to be, such as a cat, ballerina, or tree. When the sculptor lets go of the player, he tries to pose like the object mentioned and stay that way until the end of the game. When the sculptor has finished all her sculpts (meaning all players have had a spinning turn), one sculpture is chosen as the finest by the sculptor and becomes the sculptor for the next round of play.

Kongki Noli (Korea)

Kongki Noli is played by two or more players, but a small group of six or fewer is ideal. This traditional game is similar to the American game of jacks. Players take turns scattering five small pebbles (sized to fit comfortably in a player's hand) on the ground by shaking them in their hand and rolling them like dice. After they have scattered the small pebbles, round one begins. The first player picks up one of the pebbles (the "toss rock") and throws it in the air while trying to pick up one of the scattered pebbles before the toss rock touches the ground. If successful, the player picks up a second pebble, throws it in the air and tries to catch it using the same hand. If caught, she now has two pebbles in her hand and keeps throwing and catching pebble, one at a time, in the same hand, until she has caught all five pebbles. If she misses at any time, she scatters all five pebbles on the ground for the next player. The number of pebbles a player has in his hand at the end of his turn is his score for that round.

After each player has had a turn in round one, players move to round two. In the second round, a player picks up two pebbles every time she throws one up. In the third round, she picks up three and four in the fourth. The fifth time, she picks them all up. For the game's last step, a player tosses all the pebbles in the air and tries to catch them on the back of his hand. Then he tosses them up again and tries to catch them in his palm. For the final round, each player tosses all the pebbles in the air at once and tries to catch them on the back of his hand. If he misses, it is the next player's turn. If successful, he tosses them up again and tries to catch them in his palm. Players get one point for each round they complete; the player with the highest number of points at the end of all rounds wins the game.

How Many (Tanzania)

How Many needs at least six players. All players need equal amounts (fifteen to twenty) of small objects to count, such as paperclips, coins, and buttons. Without letting the other players see, the first player puts as many items in her closed fist as she chooses and puts the extra items aside so the other players cannot see them. When the objects are hidden in the player's fist, she says, "How many?" Each player has one turn to guess the exact number of objects in her hand. If a player guesses correctly, he wins the items and is able to add them to his pile. If he is wrong, he has to give her one of his objects. Players take turns hiding items and guessing until one player has all the items. The player with all of the items is the winner.

Semut, Orang, Gajah (Sumatra)

Semut, Orang, Gajah, from the Indonesian island of Sumatra, is played by two players and is similar to Rock, Paper, Scissors (pages 158–159). Players pump their fist up and down while counting to three. On four, they can give one of three signs:

- Pinky out is an ant (*semut*).
- Pointer finger out is a man (*orang*).
- Thumb out is an elephant (*gajah*).

The elephant defeats man because it is stronger. Man wins over the ant because he can step on it. The ant beats the elephant because it can crawl into the elephant's ear, bite it, or drive it crazy. If players make the same signs as each other, they go again.

Skippyroo Kangaroo (Australia)

This game needs at least six players. Players sit in a circle and select one player to be the Skippyroo (kangaroo). The Skippyroo walks to the middle of the circle and crouches on the floor with his eyes closed while the other players chant:

Skippyroo, kangaroo

Dozing in the midday sun,

Here comes a hunter, run, run, run.

Then one player from the circle touches Skippyroo's shoulder and says, "Guess who's caught you just for fun?" and then goes back into the circle. Then Skippyroo opens his eyes and tries to name the player who touched his shoulder. If he guesses correctly, they change places. If he is wrong, play continues as before with another player in the circle approaching Skippyroo. The game continues until all players have had a chance to be Skippyroo.

Jamaquack (Australia)

Jamaquack is played by a minimum of six players. Jamaquacks are rare nocturnal birds from Australia that cannot see well in daylight, so they walk aimlessly in any direction. Up to one-third of the players are Jamaquacks. The Jamaquacks must remain bent over with their hands holding their ankles and their eyes closed and can move only by walking backward during the game. All other players stand in a circle holding hands to form the Jamaquacks' pen. At the beginning of the game, the Jamaquacks gather in the middle of the pen, with their heads together. Two players drop their hands to make a hole in the pen, and the Jamaquacks begin quacking and moving backward trying to find the hole. While the Jamaquacks are trying to escape, players forming the circle do their best to move the quacks back inside the pen by gently tapping them with their knees. If the Jamaquacks escape outside the pen, they can finally stand upright and open their eyes. After Jamaquacks are outside of the circle, they should keep quacking to let the other quacks find their way out.

Yoté (West Africa)

Two players play Yoté, which has rules nearly identical to traditional checkers but is played outdoors in a sandy area. One player uses twelve small rocks as pawns, and the second player uses twelve twigs. To set up the board, players dig six rows of five holes, each large enough to fit their game pieces, but both start with their pawns (rocks or twigs) in their hand. When it's their turn, players can put a pawn on the board in a hole or can move one of their pawns already on the board forward, backward, or sideways but not diagonally. If a player's pawn is in any space next to one of his opponent's and the space on the other side is empty, he can jump it and take it off the board. The game is over when one player has four pawns left on the board and his hand is empty. The winner is the player with the most pawns taken from the other player.

Chinese Dragons (China)

Chinese Dragons needs at least six players. Players divide into two teams (it's okay if a team has one more player than the other), with one player designated as the leader on each team. Players stand in a single-file line behind their team leader and hold the waist of the player in front of them. These are the dragons. Until the "Go" signal is given by one of the team leaders, the dragons stand

> Variation: All players stand in one line, putting their hands on the shoulders of the player in front of them. The player at the front of the line is the dragon's head, and the last player is the dragon's tail. At the "Go" signal, the dragon's head tries to tag the dragon's tail. Players behind the dragon's head must keep their hands on the player in front of them and try to stop the dragon's head from catching the dragon's tail. When the dragon's head succeeds in catching the tail, the head becomes the tail and the next player at the front of the line becomes the new dragon's head.

as far from each other as possible. At the signal, only the first player, or head of each dragon, tries to tag the player at the back of the other dragon. If successful, the player at the end of the dragon joins onto the back of the dragon that tagged her, joining their team. The game ends when only one player is left on one of the dragons.

Go-Moku, Also Called Five in a Row, Go Bang, or Pegit (Japan)

Go-Moku is played by two players on a large piece of paper with a grid of fifteen rows and fifteen columns. Players take turns marking a square with their symbol, either an *O* or *X*. The first player to get five squares in a row with his symbol, horizontally, vertically, or diagonally, wins.

CHAPTER 4

CARD GAMES

> For these games, one player is the dealer and shuffles the deck before the game begins. None of the games in this section need the joker cards. These two cards should be removed and set aside before the start of any game. Unless otherwise mentioned, all games are played with a full deck of fifty-two standard playing cards.

Go Fish!

Go Fish! needs at least two players. If there are two or three players, each player receives seven cards. If there are more than three players, each player is dealt five cards. The remaining cards are placed facedown in a pile accessible to all players; this is the fish pond. Without showing anyone, players sort their cards into groups of the same number, such as a group of tens or a group of queens.

The player to the left of the dealer takes the first turn. She asks the player on her right, "Do you have an (X)?" asking for any number or face card that matches one or more she has in her hand. If the other player has this card, he must hand over all of the cards in his hand that match the request. Then the requester continues asking the same player for more cards that match a card or cards in her hand until the player does not have the cards she wants. If the player does not have the card asked for, he responds with "Go fish," and

> Variation: To keep the rules of play simpler, the game can be changed to allow players to put down a matching pair of cards, such as two eights or two kings, instead of four of a kind.

the requester picks up the top card from the fish pond pile and adds it to her hand. The player who told her to "Go fish" then becomes the new requester.

Any player collecting all four cards of a kind, such as all four twos, puts them faceup in front of him. The winner is the first player to have no cards left in his hand, only complete sets out on the table. If two people run out of cards together, the player with the most sets wins the game.

♣ Crazy Eights

Crazy Eights is played by a minimum of two players. If there are only two players, each player receives seven cards. In a game with three or more players, each player is dealt five cards. The rest of the deck is put facedown to create the draw pile. To begin, the dealer turns the top draw card faceup and places it next to the deck; this is the discard pile.

The player to the left of the dealer takes the first turn and discards a card from his hand that matches either the number or the suit of the top card on the discard pile. For example, if the top card is a two of spades, he can play any spade or any two. If he does not have a card that matches either of these, he continues to pick cards from the draw pile until he gets one that matches either the number or the suit of the top card in the discard pile. Once he has a card that can be played, he lays it down on the discard pile, and his turn is over. Eights are wild cards and can be put down at any time. For example, an eight of spades can be played to match a heart or the number five. After an eight is played, the next player must play either an eight or another card that matches the suit of the eight that was put down.

Play continues in a clockwise direction, with players taking turns matching the card at the top of the discard pile. If the draw pile runs out before the game is over, the dealer shuffles the discard pile and turns it facedown to become the new draw pile. The first player to use up all of the cards in his hand wins.

♣ War

War is for two players. One player is the dealer. The full deck of cards is dealt between the players but kept facedown in a pile in front of each player. Neither player can look at the cards.

Both players, at the same time, turn over the top card from their piles and put them faceup in the center of the table. Whoever turns over the highest-ranking card, either the highest number or highest face card, takes both cards and adds them to the bottom of his pile. Face cards are ranked in the following order (lowest to highest): jack, queen, king, ace.

Play continues in this way until two cards of the same value, such as two nines, are put down at the same time. The game is now in a state of "war." At this point, both players take two cards from the top of their piles and put one facedown and the other faceup. The player who puts down the higher-ranking faceup card wins the war and takes all cards in the center of the table. The game ends when one player is out of cards. The winner is the player with all of the cards.

Old Maid

Old Maid needs at least two players. This game is played with a standard deck of fifty-two cards with one queen removed. This leaves a pair of queens in one color and a single queen, called "the old maid," in the other color. The whole deck of cards is dealt facedown to players. It's okay if some players have more cards than others. Without showing anyone, players sort their cards into matching pairs of the same value such as jacks, queens, kings, or aces. If a player has a pair of matching cards, such as two aces or two tens of the same color, these are laid down on the table faceup. If a player has four matching cards, she puts down two pairs.

The player to the left of the dealer takes the first turn and holds all her cards up to the player on her left, making sure that only the back of the cards are visible. That player can take any card from her hand. If the new card he picks matches a card in his hand, he puts down the pair faceup. If not, he keeps it and then offers his cards to the player on his left. This continues until all cards have been put down in pairs, except the old maid or spare queen, which is left alone and cannot be paired. The player left holding this card is the old maid and loses the game.

Concentration

Concentration needs at least two players. A standard deck of fifty-two cards can be used for a more challenging game, while using fewer cards keeps the game easier. If using fewer cards, the deck needs to be made up of matching pairs. The dealer lays the cards out on a flat surface, facedown, in four equal rows.

The object of the game is to find matching pairs. Players take turns flipping two cards faceup, making sure all players have time to see the cards. If the two cards match, such as two nines or two queens, the player who flipped the cards keeps them and gets another turn. If the cards do not match, they are turned back facedown in the same place, and the next player has a turn to flip over any two cards. When all pairs have been found, players count the number of cards they have collected. The player with the most cards wins.

Snap

This game is played by a minimum of two players. Two decks of cards can be used for more than three players. The dealer distributes the full deck of cards. It's okay if some players have more cards than others. Players cannot look at their cards and have to keep them facedown in a pile in front of them.

Starting with the player to the left of the dealer, players take turns flipping over their cards, one at a time, and placing them in a pile in front of them. Play continues until a player sees two cards on top of the faceup pile of any players that are the same, such as two jacks or two sixes. The first player to see this shouts, "Snap!" and gets to keep all cards in both of the matched piles. He adds them to the bottom of his facedown pile.

If two players shout, "Snap!" at the same time, neither player gets the cards. The matching piles of cards are put side by side in the center of the playing area; this is called the "snap pool." After a snap pool is created, the two players who shouted "Snap" continue taking turns flipping their own cards faceup, one at a time until two cards match the snap pool. The player who shouts, "Snap pool!" first gets the whole pool and adds the cards to the bottom of his facedown pile. After the snap pool match is over, the game continues with all players.

If a player mistakenly shouts, "Snap!" she must give every player one card from her facedown pile. If a player has no more faceup or facedown cards, she is out of the game. The winner is the player with all the cards at the end of the game.

Variation: Each player chooses a funny animal or made-up name, such as Rocky Mountain Fuzzybird. Each player keeps his animal name for the entire game. When a player notices another player's faceup card matches his, he shouts out the name of the other player's animal three times. The first player to shout correctly wins the other player's faceup pile, which he adds to the bottom of his facedown pile. If a player calls out the wrong name, he gives three cards from his facedown pile to the player whose name he shouted incorrectly.

Rummy

Rummy requires at least two players. The object of the game is for players to get rid of cards by grouping them into "melds" or "runs." A meld is a set of three or four of a kind (such as three tens or four jacks), and a run is three or more cards in order of the same suit (such as the three, four, and five of hearts). If there are two players, each gets ten cards. If there are three or four players, each gets seven cards; five or more players get six cards each. The remaining cards are placed facedown in the middle of the playing area and become the stock pile. The top card of the stock pile is turned faceup next to it; this card begins the discard pile. Players sort cards in their hand either by suits (all hearts or spades grouped together) or according to face value (all jacks or sevens grouped together) to make it easier to see the melds and runs in their hand.

The player to the left of the dealer goes first and can take the top card from either the stock pile or the discard pile. On every turn players must draw and then discard one card to create a meld or run with the cards in their hand. After a player draws a card and discards, the player to her left takes the next turn. Play continues until a player has a meld of three or four cards of the same rank (such as three or four nines or queens) or a run of three or more cards in numerical order of the same suit (such as six, seven, eight of hearts). When it's a player's turn, if she has a meld or run in her hand, she must lay it down so it can be seen by all players. Then she discards a card faceup in the discard pile.

As soon as a meld or run is laid down, other players can put down one of their own cards, or any card they draw, if these match the meld or run. For example, a player could lay a queen down onto an existing meld of three queens. The game continues with all players drawing a card from the stock or discard pile, making melds or runs, and adding a card to the discard pile. The first player to get rid of all of his cards wins the game.

I Doubt It

I Doubt It needs a minimum of three players. The dealer passes out all cards one at a time to players facedown. It's okay if some players have more cards than others. Players look at their cards without showing other players.

The player to the left of the dealer starts the game by putting all aces she has facedown in the center of the playing area, telling all the other players what card or cards she has just played. For example, "Two aces." After the cards have been played, the game continues to the next player, who will discard all his twos. The following player discards threes, and so on. All players announce their cards as they lay them down.

Players have to play at least one card when it's their turn, even if they do not have the required card to discard. If they don't have the required card, they must still play at least one card and try to bluff what is in their hand. After a player lays her card or cards, other players can challenge her by saying, "I doubt it." When a challenge is made, the challenger looks at the discard. If the card matches what the player said, the challenger picks up all cards in the discard pile and adds them to his pile. If the cards are not what the player said they were, the player who discarded them picks up the entire discard pile. The player to lay down his entire hand first wins the game.

Slapjack

Slapjack is played by a minimum of two players. It's okay if some players have more cards than others. Players cannot look at their cards but instead must put them into a pile facedown in front of them.

The player to the left of the dealer begins by turning the card on the top of his pile faceup in the center of the table. The game continues with each player adding a card to the faceup pile. When a jack is added to the top of the pile in the center, players try to be the first to "slap" their hand over it. The player who slaps her hand on the jack first gets the entire pile and adds it to the bottom of her pile. The player to her left then starts a new faceup pile and play continues. When a player has no more cards, he has one more chance to stay in the game by slapping the next jack that appears. If he misses this opportunity, he is out of the game. The last player to have all of the cards is the winner.

> Note: The rule of slapping only the jacks needs to be understood by all players and enforced. During an exciting game, players' hands can be slapped and injured accidentally.

♣ Pig

Pig is a game for three to thirteen players. The first step is to prepare the deck of cards for play. Each player needs a set of four of a kind (cards of the same number or suit). The remaining cards are put aside and not used. If there are three players, three groups of four matching cards are needed, such as four kings, four hearts, and four threes. When it has been determined which cards will be used, the cards are shuffled and dealt so each player has four random cards. Players can look at their cards.

To begin, all players discard one card from their hand facedown on the table in front of them. When all players have put down a card, the cards are passed to the player on their left. Players pick up the new card, hoping it will match one already in their hand. This process continues until a player collects four of a kind. When a player has four of a kind, he puts his finger on his nose. If another player sees this, she puts her finger on her nose, regardless of whether or not she has four of a kind. The last player to put a finger on his nose gets a letter: first P, then I, then G. The first player to collect all three letters and spell "P-I-G" is out of the game.

♣ Chase the Ace

Chase the Ace needs a minimum of three players. Each player receives only one card, facedown. Players can peek at their cards but not show them to other players. The object of the game is to have the highest card played. Cards are ranked from ace being the lowest card to kings having the highest value.

The player to the left of the dealer can decide to keep her card or trade it by passing it facedown to the player on her left and retrieving that player's card. The only time a player does not have to trade a card with other players is when he has a king, which he must show to the other players.

Then it's the second player's turn to show her king or trade her card with the player on her left. After the exchange has taken place, the player who was forced to trade looks at his card. Then he decides if he wants to keep it or change with the player to his left. Play continues until it reaches the dealer, who cannot trade cards with any other player but can choose to trade his card for the top facedown card on the pile of unused cards. When the dealer has finished his turn, all players turn over their cards. The lowest card loses the round of play, and the player holding it loses one of three lives. Play continues until all players but one have lost all three of their lives.

Donkey

Donkey is played by at least three players. Only four cards with the same number are needed for each player. The dealer distributes cards to players one at a time, facedown. Players look at their cards without showing them to one another, sorting them into like numbers and deciding what number they will try to collect. To begin, each player chooses a card she doesn't want and puts it facedown on the table in front of her. All players together say, "One, two, three, donkey!" After the word donkey, they pass this card to the player on their right. Then each player picks up the card given to him and decides to keep or pass it along on the next turn. Players repeat the phrase and pass along cards until one player has four of a kind. When this happens, he says, "Donkey" and lays down his cards for other players to see. The first player to do so is the winner.

Rolling Stone

Rolling Stone can be played with four to six players. If there are six players, the twos are removed from the deck. With five players, twos, threes, and fours are removed from the deck. With four players, twos, threes, fours, fives, and sixes are removed from the deck. The remaining cards are shuffled and used to play the game.

The dealer passes out cards until each player has eight. After the deal, the players arrange the cards in their hand by suits. The player to the left of the dealer plays any card faceup. Play continues around the circle clockwise. The next player lays a card of the same suit, or if she does not have a card of that suit, she can pass her turn. If a player can't put down a card of that suit, she has to pick up all the faceup cards and add them to her hand. After each player has had a chance to lay a card on the pile, the player who laid down the highest card wins the round. The winner of the round starts the next round of play with a suit of his choosing. The winner of the game is the player who runs out of cards first.

♣ Sequence

Sequence needs a minimum of two players. To keep the rules of play simple, the jacks, queens, kings, and aces are removed. For more challenging play, these cards can be left in the deck. In this game, cards are ranked in numerical order with two as the lowest value, and if used, the ace as the highest card. Cards in numerical order and of the same suit make up a sequence. The dealer passes out the entire deck of cards facedown to all players. It's okay if some players have more cards than others.

The player to the left of the dealer puts her lowest card faceup on the table. Then any player who has the next card in the sequence plays it. Play continues until the ace, or highest card, of that suit is reached.

Then the next sequence begins with the player who laid the highest card on the last sequence putting down his lowest card. If at any time a player lays a card that cannot be followed (when the higher cards in that sequence have already been played), she gets another turn to lay down her lowest card. The winner is the player who is the first to get rid of all his cards.

♣ Sevens, Also Called Card Dominoes, Parliament, or Fan Tan

Sevens is played with a minimum of two players. Players pick up their hand and arrange their cards by number, lowest to highest, and by suits. The player who holds the seven of diamonds starts the game by placing this card faceup in the center of play.

The game continues with the next player to the left, who adds a diamond card to the pile either going up, such as eight, then nine, then ten, or down, such as six, then five, then four. Players take turns, in a clockwise direction, trying to add a card to the sequence pile. Cards are placed on either side of the seven so that they end up being in a row in numerical order.

If a player cannot add to the sequence, she can begin a new sequence in another suit by putting down any other seven to create a new row for that suit. If players cannot add onto an existing sequence or start a new one with a seven of any suit, they lose their turn. The winner is the first player to play all of his cards.

♣ Snip, Snap, Snorem

Snip, Snap, Snorem needs at least two players. All jacks, queens, and kings are removed from the deck. All other cards are dealt facedown, one at a time, to players. It's okay if some players have more cards than others. Players arrange their cards in their hand from lowest to highest, two being the lowest and ace being the highest.

The player to the left of the dealer starts by placing any card faceup in the center of the playing area. Next, the player to his left puts down any card of the same value on top of the card, saying "Snip." If the third player has another card of the same value, she can put it down too, saying "Snap." If at any time a player doesn't have a card to play, the play passes to the next player, and so on. The last player who puts down the final card of the set says "Snorem" and starts the next round with any card of his choice. The first player to get rid of all cards in his hand wins.

♣ Stealing Bundles, or The Old Man's Bundle

Stealing Bundles is best played with two to four players (although it can be played by up to twelve). The dealer passes out four cards facedown, one at a time, to each player. Players may look at their cards after they are dealt. Then the dealer places four cards in the center of the playing area, faceup. The rest of the deck is put aside. The player to the left of the dealer goes first and can do one of three things:

1. If she has a card or cards in her hand that are of the same value as any of the four cards in the center, she can "steal" the center card or cards and put them faceup with her own, in front of her, in a pile; this is her "bundle." If the player wins any more cards of this number or value in another turn, they go on the top of this bundle, with only the top card showing.

2. If she has a card of the same value as the top card in another player's bundle, she can steal all cards in that player's bundle, add her matching cards, and put them faceup as a bundle in front of her.

3. If she has no cards matching the ones in the center or another player's bundle, she discards a card by putting it faceup in the center. This adds more cards for her opponent to choose from. Or if she has no cards matching the ones in the center or another player's bundle, she starts a "trail" by putting one of her cards faceup in the center.

Cards are kept in separate bundles according to their face value or numeral. When all players have played all four of their original cards, four new cards are dealt to all players from the deck, and the game continues. When all cards have been dealt and played, the player with the most bundles wins.

♣ The Great Wall of Cards

The Great Wall of Cards is played with a minimum of two players. The dealer passes out all cards so each player has an equal number. Any extra cards are not used. Players stand up and take turns tossing their cards, one at a time, at the base of a wall. The goal is to get a card to land straight or leaning against the wall instead of landing flat on the floor. A player whose card lands this way gets to keep the "pot," or all of the cards already thrown. Cards collected from the pot are kept facedown in a pile and separate from the cards in a player's hand. The game continues until all cards in players'

> **Variation:** For less-skilled players, a card tossed so it lands faceup wins the pot. A more challenging rule is to designate a suit as the only one that can take the pot, such as only a card with a spade or heart being able to win.

hands have been tossed. The winner is the player with the most cards in his pile.

Egyptian Ratscrew, Also Called Egyptian War

Egyptian Ratscrew needs two to five players. The dealer passes out all cards facedown so that all players have an equal number; any remaining cards are stacked faceup in the middle of the playing area as bonus cards. After the cards are dealt, players stack their hand facedown in front of them without looking at the cards.

The player to the left of the dealer takes the top card from his stack without looking at it and quickly lays it faceup on the center pile. If the card laid has a value of two through ten, play continues with the player to his left laying the top card from her pile onto the center pile and so on. However, if a player lays a face card (jack, queen, king) or ace on the pile, the player to her left must try to lay a face card on top of it. The number of tries that player gets to play a face card depends on the original card played. For jacks she gets only one try, for queens two tries, for kings three tries, and for aces four tries.

If the player is able to play a face card, play moves to the next player, and he must put another face card on the pile. If he cannot, the player who put down the last face card wins the pile. For instance, if a player has a queen played to her and she goes through two of her cards without putting down a face card, then the player who played the queen wins all the cards in the pile. The first player to get all cards in his pile wins the game.

Salute the King

Salute the King needs at least three players. With eight or more players, it's best to use two decks of cards. Incomplete decks can also be used to increase the total card count. The only cards that affect the game are the ace, king, queen, and jack. Players must know the appropriate actions prior to the start of the game.

- Ace: All players stand up.
- King: All players salute.

- Queen: All players put their hand over their heart and bow while remaining seated.
- Jack: All players start clapping.

After there are enough cards for play, the entire deck of cards is dealt facedown one at a time. It's okay if some players have more cards than others. Cards are kept facedown in front of each player and are turned over only when it's a player's turn.

Starting with the player to the left of the dealer, all players turn over their top card one by one and put it in the middle of the playing area. When each card is turned over, all players gesture as quickly as possible according to the face value of the card.

For example, when a king is turned over and put in the middle of the playing area, all players salute. The last player to salute loses the round and has to take all cards from the center pile. Because this is a fast-paced game, players may forget which gestures they are supposed to do. If a player does an incorrect gesture, she must pick up the center pile. The first player to get rid of all of his cards is the winner.

♣ Hit the Hat

Hit the Hat requires a minimum of two players and a hat of any kind. The dealer groups cards according to their suits. The hat is placed open-side up on the floor. Players can either sit or stand around it. The dealer passes out all cards so that each player has an equal number. Any extra cards are set aside and not used. If there are four players or fewer, each player should have all cards in one suit, such as player one has all of the diamonds, and player two gets all of the spades.

Players take turns trying to throw all their cards into the hat. The distance from the hat can be adjusted to meet the skill level of the players. After each round of play, all of the cards on the floor are returned to the player who threw them. The first player to get all of his cards in the hat is the winner. To make this easier, a wastebasket, large box, or bucket instead of a hat can help players be more successful.

♣ Spit

Spit is played with two players. The dealer passes out cards facedown and equally to both players. Players may not look at their cards before they are played. After the deal, each player creates five piles of cards facedown in front of her. The first pile has only one card; the second pile has two cards; third pile, three cards; fourth pile, four cards; and fifth pile, five cards. Then the top card of each pile is turned faceup. The players' extra eleven cards become their stockpile and are placed in front of them, facedown.

When both players are ready to start the game, they simultaneously yell, "Spit," and flip over a card from their stockpile, placing them side by side in the middle of the playing area. These cards become the first cards of the spit piles. After the spit piles are created, the object of the game is to move the faceup cards from the top of their five piles onto a spit pile as fast as they can. Players simultaneously move quickly, using only one hand to move one card at a time from their piles onto the spit piles. There's no need to be polite and take turns in this game.

For players to move a card from one of their five piles onto a spit pile, their card must be next in sequence (either one rank higher or one rank lower; suits don't matter) than the card on the top of a spit pile. The spit piles change rapidly, as each player slaps a new card on them. If both players cannot put a card on a spit pile, they yell, "Spit!" again and flip a card from their stockpile on the spit piles at the same time. Play continues until one player is out of cards.

Note: In addition to using playing cards for games, they are equally fun to use for construction projects. The simplest is a triangle or two-card arch. After players get familiar with how cards must be placed and propped together, more elaborate architectural structures can be designed. To make the construction projects easier, builders can cut notches along the sides of the cards so they fit and hold together firmly, making the structures more stable.

♣ Authors

Authors is played with three to five players. The dealer passes out all cards facedown, one at a time. It's okay if some players have more cards than others. Players arrange their cards in their hand according to their numerical or face value. The object of the game is to collect as many four-of-a-kind sets as possible.

The player to the left of the dealer starts by choosing another player and asking her for a specific card, such as the seven of hearts. The player asking for a card must be holding at least one card of the same value in his hand to ask for it. If the player gets the card he asks for, he gets another turn and is able to ask again. If he does not get the card, the next player (to his left) gets a turn to ask for a card.

When a player collects four cards of a kind, she shows them to the other players and places them faceup in a pile front of her. When a player runs out of cards, he is out of the game and waits while the other players finish playing their cards. When all of the cards have been played, the player with the most sets of four cards wins the game.

♣ Guess and Win

Guess and Win needs either two or three players. The dealer passes out all cards, one at a time to each player, facedown. It doesn't matter if some players have more cards than others at the start. Players may not look at their cards.

The player to the left of the dealer goes first. Players take turns placing their top card faceup in a pile in the middle of the playing area. Just before flipping over their card, they guess out loud a

---

Note: Card games are often more fun when players make up their own rules. To keep the games simple, players can create their own game of grouping cards by colors, suits, numbers, or faces. Cards can be arranged in numerical order or used for mathematical functions such as addition, subtraction, multiplication, or division. The possibilities are endless—so are the rules. Card Bingo anyone?

number or face value, trying to predict what their card will not be. If a player makes a prediction and the card she turns over matches the prediction, she takes all cards from the pile. If the prediction does not match, the next player takes a turn. The first player without cards is the winner.

CHAPTER 5

CLAPPING GAMES

Down, Down Baby

In Down, Down Baby, two or more players stand in a circle and clap in tune to this rhyming song:

Down, down, baby, (Players clap one another's hands four times.)

Down, down the roller coaster. (Players clap twice and then make a horizontal wave motion with both hands.)

Sweet, sweet, baby, (Players clap one another's hands four times.)

I'll never let you go. (Players shake their head and their pointer fingers.)

Shimmy, shimmy cocoa pop, (Players clap one another's hands four times.)

Shimmy, shimmy pow. (Players clap twice; then on the word pow, players lift their hands in the air.)

Shimmy, shimmy cocoa pop, (Players clap one another's hands four times.)

Shimmy, shimmy pow. (Players clap twice; then on the word pow, players lift their hands in the air.)

Miss Mary Mack

Miss Mary Mack is perhaps the most common hand-clapping game in the United States. In the game, two players stand or sit facing each other and clap their hands or those of their partner in time to the chant below:

Miss Mary Mack, Mack, Mack,

All dressed in black, black, black

With silver buttons, buttons, buttons

All down her back, back, back.

She asked her mother, mother, mother

For fifty cents, cents, cents

To see the elephants, elephants, elephants

Jump the fence, fence, fence.

They jumped so high, high, high,

They reached the sky, sky, sky

And didn't come back, back, back

'Til the 4th of July, -ly, -ly!

She asked her mother, mother, mother

For five cents more, more, more

To see the elephants, elephants, elephants

Jump over the door, door, door.

They jumped so low, low, low,

They stubbed their toe, toe, toe

And that's the end, end, end,

Of the elephant show, show, show!

In addition to hand claps, players can add hand gestures and body movements according to the words in the chant.

Pat-a-Cake, or Patty Cake

Pat-a-Cake is among the first clapping games played with babies. Typically, the baby is held by an adult who helps him clap his hands. As the baby gets older, he can copy the adult's motions during this game. Hand movements are simple and vary widely. Here is one common version:

Pat-a-cake, pat-a-cake, baker's man. (An adult holds the baby's

hands and claps them.)

Bake me a cake as fast as you can.

Pat it and shape it and mark it with "B" (or initial of the baby's

name). (An adult uses the baby's pointer finger to make the

letter.)

And bake it in the oven for baby and me. (An adult takes both of

the baby's hands and gently moves them in a push-off motion.)

Other common lyrics:

Patty cake, patty cake, baker's man.

Bake me a cake as fast as you can.

Roll it up, roll it up,

And toss it in a pan!

Patty cake, patty cake, baker's man.

Peas Porridge Hot

In Peas Porridge Hot, two players sit facing each other with their knees touching. The lyrics and hand movements are as follows:

Peas porridge hot, (Both players slap their thighs, clap their

hands, and clap their partner's hands.)

Peas porridge cold, (Players repeat previous motions.)

Peas porridge in the pot, (Both players slap their thighs, clap their hands, clap their partner's right hand, and then clap their hands.)

Nine days old. (Players clap their partner's left hand, clap their hands, then clap both their partner's hands.)

Some like it hot, (Both players slap their thighs, clap their hands, and then clap their partner's hands.)

Some like it cold. (Players repeat motions from the line above.)

Some like it in the pot, (Both players slap their thighs, clap their hands, clap their partner's right hand, then clap their hands.)

Nine days old (Players clap their partner's left hand, clap their own hands, and then clap both their partner's hands.)

Miss Susie Had a Baby

Miss Susie Had a Baby requires two players sitting or standing facing each other. Hand motions can vary, but typically, players clap own hands and those of their partner in a repetitive manner. Players can create their own clapping patterns, hand gestures, and movements, which is part of the fun of this game. The lyrics to be sung or chanted are as follows:

Miss Susie had a baby.

His name was Tiny Tim, Tim, Tim.

She put him in the bathtub

To see if he could swim, swim, swim.

He drank up all the water.

He ate up all the soap.

He tried to eat the bathtub,

But it wouldn't go down his throat, throat, throat.

Miss Susie called the doctor.

The doctor called the nurse.

The nurse called the lady

With the alligator purse.

Out ran the doctor.

Out ran the nurse.

Out ran the lady

With the alligator purse.

And now Tiny Tim

Is home sick in bed,

With soap in his throat

And bubbles in his head.

 ## Grandma, Grandma Sick in Bed

Grandma, Grandma Sick in Bed includes both hand claps and body movements. It can be chanted and played by a group or just one player. Some suggested clapping patterns and movements are:

Grandma, Grandma sick in bed,

She called the doctor and the doctor said,

Let's get the rhythm of the head, ding-dong. (Players rock their head to each side once in time with "ding-dong.")

Let's get the rhythm of the head, ding-dong. (Players rock their head to each side once in time with "ding-dong.")

Let's get the rhythm of the hands. (Players clap one another's hands twice, followed by two hand claps.)

Let's get the rhythm of the hands. (Players clap one another's hands twice, followed by two hand claps.)

Let's get the rhythm of the feet. (Players stomp their right foot, then their left.)

Let's get the rhythm of the feet. (Players stomp their right foot, then their left.)

Let's get the rhythm of the hot dog. (Players place their hands on their hips and twirl.)

Let's get the rhythm of the hot dog. (Players place their hands on their hips and twirl.)

Put it all together, and what do you get?

Ding-dong, (Players rock their head, followed by two claps and then two foot stomps.)

Hot dog. (Players circle their hips.)

Put it all backward and what do you get?

Hot dog, (Players twirl their hips followed by two stomps and then two claps.)

Ding-dong. (Players rock their head.)

Bingo

Bingo can be chanted and played by a group or just one player. Players add an additional hand clap to each verse of the chant. The word "clap" in the second through fifth verses indicates that players clap their hands instead of saying a letter. For instance, in the second verse, players clap their hands instead of saying "B."

There was a farmer had a dog,

And Bingo was his name-o.

B-I-N-G-O!

B-I-N-G-O!

B-I-N-G-O!

And Bingo was his name-o!

There was a farmer had a dog,

And Bingo was his name-o.

(Clap)-I-N-G-O!

(Clap)-I-N-G-O!

(Clap)-I-N-G-O!

And Bingo was his name-o!

There was a farmer had a dog,

And Bingo was his name-o.

(Clap, clap)-N-G-O!

(Clap, clap)-N-G-O!

(Clap, clap)-N-G-O!

And Bingo was his name-o!

There was a farmer had a dog,

And Bingo was his name-o.

(Clap, clap, clap)-G-O!

(Clap, clap, clap)-G-O!

(Clap, clap, clap)-G-O!

And Bingo was his name-o!

There was a farmer had a dog,

And Bingo was his name-o.

(Clap, clap, clap, clap)-O!

(Clap, clap, clap, clap)-O!

(Clap, clap, clap, clap)-O!

And Bingo was his name-o!

There was a farmer had a dog,

And Bingo was his name-o.

(Clap, clap, clap, clap, clap)

(Clap, clap, clap, clap, clap)

(Clap, clap, clap, clap, clap)

And Bingo was his name-o!

In a Cabin in the Woods

In a Cabin in the Woods can be chanted and played by a group or just one player. Each player uses the same hand motions while chanting the words:

In a cabin in the woods, (Players draw a square in the air with their fingers.)

A little old man by the window stood, (Players make circles, like binoculars, with their hands and put them up to their eyes.)

Saw a rabbit hopping by. (Players use two fingers hopping in the air in front of them.)

Knocking at his door, (Players make a knocking motion with one hand.)

"Help me! Help me! Help me!" he cried, (Players throw their hands up in the air three times.)

"'Fore the hunter shoot me down." (Players point an imaginary gun with both hands and move side to side.)

"Come, little rabbit, come inside. (Players make a hand motion inviting someone to come inside.)

Happy we will always be." (Players hug themselves and rock back and forth.)

This chant is repeated multiple times. Each time the chant is said, players hum a line (instead of saying the words in that line), as they do the hand gestures. For instance, the second time the chant is said, players don't say "In a cabin in the woods," they just hum it and make the hand gesture. The third time, players leave out both first and second lines, humming only while doing the hand gestures. Then they continue saying the rest of the chant. This pattern continues until there are no words, just humming and gestures.

Bo-Bo

Bo-Bo is a clapping game in which players can either clap the hands of a partner or their own hands. The fun of this game is for players to make up their own clapping rhythms, hand motions, and lyrics at the end of the chant.

Bo-bo ski watten tatten,

Ah-ah-ah, boom boom boom.

Itty-bitty watten tatten,

Bo-bo ski watten tatten,

Bo-bo ski watten tatten,

Freeze please American cheese. (Players stop clapping.)

Please don't show your teeth to me. (Players resume clapping.)

This chant can be repeated with the last line changed to "Please don't show your eyes to me," and so on.

CHAPTER 6

DICE GAMES

Dice games are for two or more players. They help develop a variety of skills, including number awareness, manual dexterity, verbal language, and socialization through healthy competition and rules of fair play. In all dice games, players take turns rolling and then passing the dice to the player on their left.

 Don't Be Greedy

Only one die is needed for Don't Be Greedy. The first player rolls the die for as many turns as she chooses. Every time the player throws the die, she adds the number from the die to her total score. Players can continue to roll or stop and take their points at any time. If a one is rolled, the player loses all of the points she has accumulated from that round. Players take turns throwing the die, adding points to their total score or losing all points if they throw a one. The first player to reach fifty points (or more) is the winner.

Variation: This game can also be played with two dice. A player is awarded the points from his throw as long as he does not throw a one on either die. If a player rolls a double, he doubles his score for that throw. For example: if the player throws a double four, that adds up to eight points, multiplied by two, makes sixteen points for that throw.

High Dice

In High Dice, one player is the banker and throws two dice. He adds the total of the two dice together and that is his score. Other players take turns throwing the dice to see if anyone can throw a higher score than the banker. A player who throws a score higher than the banker receives a point. If a player rolls the same score or less than the banker, she doesn't get a point. If no player throws higher than the banker, the banker gets one point. After everyone has had a chance to roll the dice, the banker rolls again and creates a new score to beat. The player or banker who gets ten points first is the winner.

Ready? Roll!

Ready? Roll! is played by three or more players. Two dice and three small objects such as paperclips or coins are needed as counters for this game. Players sit in a circle on the floor facing one another, with the three counters in the middle. The game begins with two players each having a die. The players without dice slap their thighs once, then clap their hands once, repeating this pattern to create a beat. When all players are following the rhythm, they chant as follows, with each line of the chant taking one set of slap/clap:

> *Are you*
>
> *Ready?*
>
> *Are you*
>
> *Ready?*
>
> *If*
>
> *So,*
>
> *Let's*
>
> *Go!*
>
> *Roll now!*
>
> *What have you got?*

Must you pass?

Hope not!

At the "Roll now!" command, the players with dice roll once, trying not to get a six. If a player throws a six, he passes his die to the player on his left and joins the chant for the next round. If no six is thrown, the players retain their dice and the chant starts again. A player wins the round and collects a counter when she is still in possession of a die, and the other player has to pass his die to the next player. After the last counter has been grabbed from the middle of the circle, the player with the most counters wins.

> Variation: If there are six or eight players, the passing roll is increased to two numbers, such as a five and a six. This can speed the game up considerably.

Beat That

Two or more dice are used for Beat That, depending on the age and ability of the players. The first player rolls the dice and arranges them next to each other, in order to make the highest number possible. For example, if a two and five are rolled, the highest number possible is fifty-two. If using three dice, a roll of six, four, and one can be arranged to be 641. The player writes down his number, passes the dice to the player on his left and says "Beat That!" After each player has had a turn to roll, the player with the highest number wins that round of play and gets one point. The game continues until a player gets ten points.

> Variations: Players arrange dice to make the smallest number possible with the smallest number earning the point. For a more challenging game, up to seven dice can be used.

Easy Does It

Easy Does It can be played with one or two dice. Before the game begins, each player chooses a different number from one to six, if using one die, or from two to twelve, if two dice are used. Players take turn rolling. If a player rolls the number she chose at the beginning of the game, she gets a point and another roll. If she does not roll her number, she passes the dice to the player on her left, and the next player has a turn. All players keep track of their scores. The first player to get ten points wins.

> Variation: The point total can be adjusted. To make it easier for a player to win, lowering the point count needed to win will help players be more successful, while a higher point count is more challenging.

Triples

Triples is a simple game with three dice. Players take turns rolling all three dice at once. The winner is the player who first gets a three of a kind.

Going to Town

Three dice are needed for Going to Town. The first player rolls all three dice and sets aside the die with the highest number. Then he rolls the remaining two dice and again sets aside the highest number, then the third and last die. The player then adds all three numbers and writes it on his score sheet. After he has added his score, he passes the dice to the player on his left to have the next turn. Players continue to take turns rolling the dice and adding their score from each round together. The first player to reach a predetermined number of points wins the game.

Ladder

Ladder is played with two dice. Before the game, each player draws a ladder with six rungs on a sheet of paper with the numbers one to six on both sides of the rungs, starting at the bottom. Players take turns throwing the dice. As the numbers are thrown, they are crossed off the left side of the ladder, and the dice are passed to the next player. For example, if a player throws a two and a four, those numbers are crossed off the left side of her ladder and dice given to the next player. All numbers on the left side of the ladder must be crossed off before a player can cross off numbers on the right side of the ladder. The winner is the first player to have all numbers on both sides of the ladder crossed off.

> **Variations:** To make the game more challenging, players can cross off the numbers on the ladder only in numerical order, such as the one must be crossed off before the two can be. For older players, up to twelve rungs can be used. The value of one die or total value of both dice thrown by a player can be added together to help players cross off numbers on their ladders.

Stuck in the Mud

A piece of paper and five dice are needed for Stuck in the Mud. The goal of this game is to not roll a two or a five. The first player rolls all five dice. If he rolls a two or a five, those dice are set aside, and the player does not score any points for that roll. He may take the remaining dice that have not been set aside and try to roll again, trying to avoid a two or a five. If the player does not roll a two or a five, he adds up the total number of dots showing on the dice and puts this score on his tally sheet. The player continues rolling dice, setting aside any die showing a two or a five or counting total points (if a two or a five is not showing) until all five dice have been set aside. When all five dice are out, that player is "stuck in the mud," and all dice are passed to the next player so she can roll and accumulate points until she is "stuck in the mud" too. After all players are stuck in the mud, the player with the highest number of points wins the game.

Fifty

In Fifty, players take turns rolling two dice trying to get the same number on each die (a double). Players score points only when they get a double. The score depends on the double numbers on the dice. Every double one, two, three, four, or five scores as five points. Double sixes count as twenty-five points. The first player to reach fifty points wins the game.

> Variation: To make the game more challenging, players lose all the points they have accumulated when they roll a double three.

'Round the Clock

Each player needs two dice in 'Round the Clock. All players simultaneously roll their two dice, trying to roll numbers around the clock. On the first roll, players are trying to get one or both dice to have a one. Players keep rolling until they are successful and roll a one. Then they roll again, hoping for a two on their next turn. They can count either a die with a face number of two or two ones, which add up to two. Again, they roll until they are successful and then roll for the number three on their next turn. The game continues with players trying for numbers one through twelve, in numerical order. For example, a player cannot try for a five until he gets a die with a four or two dice that add to four when combined. The first player to throw all numbers from one to twelve in order wins the game and has gone 'Round the Clock.

Knockout

Before Knockout starts, players choose six, seven, eight, or nine as their "knockout" number. More than one player can have the same knockout number. Then players take turns rolling two dice. On each turn, the face numbers of the player's rolled dice are added together. If the total is equal to the knockout number, that player is knocked out. The winner is the last player not knocked out.

Three or More

In Three or More, players take turns rolling five dice at a time. The goal of the game is to get three of a kind or higher to earn points. Players getting three of a kind earn three points, four of a kind scores six points, and five of a kind scores twelve points.

If a player gets only two of a kind or no matches, she can throw the remaining dice one more time trying to get more points. If she's not successful, she does not earn any points. Players keep track of their scores. The player with the highest total score after five rounds wins the game.

 ## Twenty-One

In Twenty-One, players take turns rolling two dice and adding the total of the dice. Each player can continue rolling and adding points until he chooses to stop. The goal is to get the highest total number of points without going over twenty-one. If a player gets more than twenty-one, he is out of the game. If there is a tie for the highest total number of points, those players have a playoff round. The winner is the player with the highest total under twenty-one. Each round of play starts with a different player, to give everyone an equal chance to win.

CHAPTER 7

GAMES TO PLAY WHILE YOU WAIT

 ### The Hunt

The Hunt is played by two or more players in one-minute rounds. One player chooses a letter of the alphabet and shares it with all the players. During the time limit, players write down all of the objects they see starting with the chosen letter. To make the game easier for young players, players can be allowed to draw the objects or whisper them to someone who writes them down. The player with the most objects written down at the end of one minute is the winner and gets to choose the letter for the next round of play.

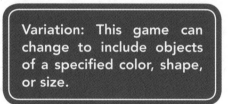

Variation: This game can change to include objects of a specified color, shape, or size.

 ### Tell Me a Story

Tell Me a Story needs two or more players. Picture books are often located in waiting areas, so this is a perfect game to play using any book that's available. One player reads a picture book to the other players. When finished, the listeners take turns telling the story in their own words, using only the pictures in the book as a guide. If books are not available, one player can make up a story and ask others to tell it back.

Wacky World

Wacky World is played by two or more players and encourages creativity. Players take turns creating their own wacky world by designing places, animals, and people far from reality. To play the game, one player asks the other players, "What would happen if . . ." For example, a player can ask, "What would happen if parents became the children, and the children became the parents?" or "What would happen if everyone lived in airplanes that never landed?" The other players take turns answering the question. After everyone has given an answer, another player has a turn asking a question. Although these are fanciful questions, answers are often creative or occasionally even logical.

What Do You Do?

The What Do You Do? guessing game needs at least two players. One player chooses a profession without telling other players what it is. Then players take turns asking only yes or no questions trying to guess what the job is, such as, "Do you use a hammer?" or "Do you cook food?" If the players cannot guess the correct occupation after every player has asked two yes or no questions, they can ask for a demonstration. At this time, the first player must silently act out one or more job tasks. The player to answer correctly gets the next turn to think of a job for the others to guess.

Telephone

Telephone needs at least four players. All players sit in a circle. The first player thinks of a short message and whispers the message to the player on his right side. When that player receives the message, she immediately whispers what she thinks she heard to the player to her right. The whispers continue until everyone in the circle gets the message. The last player to

Variations: For a simpler version, players are put in pairs instead of a large group with the first player whispering a simple word to the next player, who then repeats the word as soon as she hears it. For a more complicated game, use a complete sentence or nonsense phrase, such as "holy moly, guacamole." In another version, a phrase to be acted out by the last player is whispered around the circle.

receive the message tells the group what he heard. The final message is typically not at all what the first player said. Then the game continues with a new player starting a new message.

Guess What I Found?

Guess What I Found? is played by two or more players. One player is the leader. While all players shut their eyes, the leader takes an item out of a purse, bag, pocket, or wallet. With their eyes still closed, players take turns feeling the object and guessing what it is. The first player to correctly guess the item wins the game and has the next turn to choose an object.

> Variations: To make the game more challenging, after the object is guessed, it is returned to the purse or bag, and players try to find it only by feeling objects in the bag with their eyes closed. If the game is played without a purse or bag, the object is hidden somewhere nearby so that it is only partly visible. Then players look for it while still seated. The first player to locate the object is the winner and has a turn to find another object for the next round of play.

Guess How Many

Two or more players can play Guess How Many. One player hides coins (or other small objects such as pebbles or paper clips) in one of her hands and asks the other players one at a time,

> Note: This game is not appropriate for children under three, due to the choking hazard of the small objects used for play.

"Guess how many." After all players have taken a guess, the player who guesses the correct answer or is closest to exact number is the winner and has the next turn to hide the objects. If two players guess the correct answer, a playoff round determines the winner.

Create an Animal

Create an Animal needs three or more players. Before beginning, one player chooses a class of animals for the round of play, such as birds, fish, mammals, insects, reptiles, or amphibians. To simplify the game, a player can choose where the animals live, such as in the water, on ground, underground, or in the sky. Then each player creates an imaginary animal from the chosen class with a unique look, unusual name, strange diet, and special way to communicate and takes a turn telling about his animal. Every player who participates is a winner. After all players have had a chance to tell about and act out their animal, another player chooses a new class of animals for the next round of play.

> Variation: Each player creates an animal by having two parents from different species. For instance, what would an animal be called with a mother who is a woodpecker and a father who is a robin? The answer might be a woodin or a robpecker. What would they sound like? Possibilities are so much fun to imagine. If drawing materials are available, players can sketch their animals.

What's Happening?

What's Happening? is played by two or more players. One player is the leader and chooses an interesting photo in a magazine or picture book and gives other players time to look carefully at it while she counts slowly and quietly to fifty (or more). Then the leader holds the photo so the other players can't see it, and they take turns describing it in a sentence or phrase. Each player has a turn to add something new to the description of the photo given by other players. If players get stuck, the leader can ask questions about the photo (according to the age or abilities of the players) such as, "How many cars were there?" or "What was the little boy doing?" To make this game more challenging, the leader can ask questions about something that was not in the photo. For example, if the photo included only children, the leader can ask how many adults there were. When Q&A time is up, the photo is shown to everyone again. This game doesn't have a winner, but it could be made competitive by keeping track of the number of correct descriptions of each photo.

Thumb Wrestling

Thumb Wrestling is between two players. Both players face each other and place their right thumb in mid-air. With their right-hand fingertips, they grab their opponent's right-hand fingertips tightly. Players start with a beginning thumb flex (bow) and then chant, "One, two, three, four, I declare a thumb war!" Then the wrestling begins. The winner is the first one to pin the other player's thumb down for five counts while keeping his fingertips clasped together.

I Spy with My Little Eye

I Spy with My Little Eye is played with three or more players. Player one secretly picks something she sees and says, "I spy with my little eye something . . ." and gives a hint that can include the size, color, shape, or use of the item. Players take turns guessing the item. The first player to guess correctly chooses for the next round.

Twenty Questions

This game is played with two or more players. One player chooses an item, a person, or a place all players know, and the other players take turns asking up to twenty questions that can be answered only with a yes or no. During a turn, a player can take a chance and guess what the item is. If he guesses correctly, he can choose a new item for the next round of play, but if he guesses incorrectly, he is out of the game until the next round.

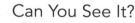

Can You See It?

The Can You See It? guessing game needs at least three players. One player is the leader. The leader describes one attribute of an item visible to all players, such as texture (hard, soft, bumpy, or smooth), size, color, use, or shape. Then players look around for items with this attribute. Each player takes turns naming a different object with the chosen quality until no players can add to the list. The last player to add an object to the list chooses the next category.

Things Aren't What They Seem

Things Aren't What They Seem is played with three or more players. One player is the leader and chooses an object found in a purse, bag, or pocket or an object that is visible to all players, such as a clock, ballpoint pen, telephone, or keys. The leader tells the other players what the object is and starts an imaginative story about it. Then players take turns adding to the story started by the leader. The story must not be typical of the object but must have a new and different use for it. For example, if the leader chooses a set of keys for a house or a car, the player may say something like, "These keys are for a palace where a goofy wizard lives with his beautiful princess wife and sixteen children." The next player who adds to this story may say, "The keys open the door to a room full of frogs doing cartwheels." Players continue adding on to the story until one player says "The End" and starts another story.

Picture Puzzle

Picture Puzzle needs a minimum of three players and is best played when magazines with large photos or picture books are available. One player is the leader. The leader covers at least half of a photo or illustration with a blank piece of paper and asks the other players to take turns guessing what it is. To make the game easier, the leader can leave more of the photo exposed; it's more challenging when only a small portion of the photo is shown. The

Variation: One player flips through a magazine or book until finding a photo or illustration. When she has found a photo, the player closes the magazine, remembering the image. Then other players try to find that photo or illustration based on hints given by that player. The first player to find the correct photo chooses the photo for the next round.

first player to guess the photo correctly gets to choose a photo for the next round. It may be necessary to keep revealing more of the photo until someone figures out what the photo is.

Categories

Categories is played with three or more players. One player selects a category, such as animals, vehicles, countries, or things that taste good, and tells the category to the other players. Then players take turns naming an item that belongs to that category. A player is out of the game when he cannot think of a new item to add. The last player to successfully add a word is the winner and selects the category for the next round of play.

> Variation: To make the game more challenging, players' answers must be in alphabetical order. For example, if "animals" is the category, the answers could be ant, bee, and cow.

Would You Rather?

Would You Rather? needs two or more players. One player is the leader, who starts by asking a simple "Would you rather . . ." question, such as "Would you rather play baseball or a card game?" "Eat an apple or a pear?" "Take a bath or a shower?" or "Have a picnic with an anteater or a raccoon?" Players take turns answering the question. After a player gives his answer, the leader asks, "Why?" The sillier the reasons, the better. After all players have had a turn to answer the question, the leader chooses what she considers the best answer. Then that player becomes the new leader for the next round of play.

Silent Monkey See, Monkey Do

Silent Monkey See, Monkey Do needs three or more players. One player is the monkey and silently makes faces, gestures, or actions while looking at other players. The other players watch the monkey and try not to show any emotion. Any player who laughs or smiles is out of that round of play. The last player to laugh or smile gets the next turn to be the silly but silent monkey.

What Am I?

What Am I? can be played by two or more players. The first player picks an item that is visible to all of the players and gives clues to describe it while the other players take turns guessing what it is. For example, hints may be, "I am on the top shelf and live in a green box." The first player who spots the item wins the round and gets to choose the next item.

Never Stop Moving

Never Stop Moving is a way to pass time while standing in line. All players must be moving and taking steps the entire time they are waiting in line. Players should take the smallest steps possible and not stop until reaching the front of the line. If the line is moving slowly, players can move in any direction, with no need to follow behind another player.

Picture This

Picture This needs two or more players and a cell phone with a camera that can zoom. Players turn their back or close their eyes while one player takes a close-up photo of something visible to all players. Then this photo is shared with the other players, who take turns guessing what the item is. The first player with the correct answer is the winner and becomes the photographer for the next round.

Rhyme Time

Rhyme Time is played with three or more players. One player names a person, object, animal, place, or food known by everyone playing the game. Other players take turns saying a word that rhymes with the chosen word without repeating a word already mentioned by another player. When no one can think of more rhyming words, a new player chooses a word, and the game starts again.

Variation: Instead of a rhyming word, players match the beginning sounds of a word within the category of people, objects, animals, food, or places. For instance, if the word chosen is "Mom," players say a person word that starts with an "M," such as Martha, Martin, and Megan.

Words, Words

Words, Words needs at least three players. One player picks a word that names an object such as ball, cup, boat, or box. Other players take turns adding a descriptive word or phrase that includes the chosen word. For example, if "cup" is the chosen word, other players could say "measuring cup," "teacup," or "paper cup." Play continues until no player can add to the list of descriptive words already mentioned. The last player to add a word has a turn to choose a new word and start the next round of play. Acceptable descriptive words or phrases must be ones commonly used, known by all players, or add definition to the chosen word. Descriptive words that include size, color, or numbers (such as "blue cup") are not acceptable or counted as a correct answer.

Variation: An easier version for players with less vocabulary is to select a category and name items within that category such as foods that taste good, modes of transportation, or the names of birds or fish. The last player to add a word chooses the word for the next round of play.

Oh, Say Can You See?

Oh, Say Can You See? is played with three or more players in an area where there are signs with letters on them. One player is the leader. The leader says or sings, "Oh, say can you see the letter (D)?" Other players take turns looking for signs with the letter D, and when it's their turn, point these out to everyone. The game ends when the last player finds a sign with the chosen letter; he gets to choose the new letter for the next round of play.

Variation: When players know their letters and beginning sounds, the game can be changed to find objects that start with the letter chosen.

Simon Says

Simon Says needs at least three players. One player is Simon and tells the other players what they must do. Players must follow Simon's directions, but only if he begins his commands with "Simon says." If Simon does not begin his commands in this way, players do not obey. Any player who does so is out of the game. Some good commands include, "wiggle your nose," "wink (or blink) five times," "roll your tongue," "clap using only two fingers," "stand on your heels," or "stand on your toes." When only one player is left obeying Simon, she is the winner and becomes the new Simon for the next round of play.

Animal Antics

Animal Antics is played with three or more players. This game is much like Charades, except simpler to do while waiting in a line. One player is the leader and chooses an animal, telling the other players only where this animal typically lives, such as in a jungle, on the farm, or as a pet. Next the leader acts out the animal for the others. Other players take turns guessing what the animal is, based on the sounds or movements. The round ends when a player correctly guesses the animal. That player gets to choose an animal for the next round.

Move Over, Dr. Seuss

Move Over, Dr. Seuss needs three or more players, who create silly words and then define them. The leader thinks of any word and shares it with the group. Then other players take turns saying words, either real or imaginary, that rhyme with the chosen word and give those words a definition. The first player starts with the letter A. Then each player adds a rhyming word, starting with the next letter in the alphabet. For example, if the leader chooses the word "dog," the first player has to think of a word that rhymes with it, beginning with A, such as "afog" and then makes up a definition for the word: "'Afog' is when you can't see anything outside." The next player thinks of a rhyming word starting with B. If a player cannot think of a word when it's his turn, he simply says "Pass," and the next player gets a chance to add her word to the growing list of silly words. The game ends when the original word has been rhymed with all letters in the alphabet. At that time, a new player is the leader, and a new word is selected to rhyme.

Back to Writing

Back to Writing is best played in pairs. Both players stand single file, one in front of the other. The player in the back uses one of her fingers to draw a letter, number, shape, or word on the back of the player in front of her. The player in front guesses what image was drawn on his back. If the player guesses correctly, the players switch roles, but if the player's guess was incorrect, the player in back continues drawing until a correct answer is given.

> Variation: More advanced artists can draw an object on their partner's back.

Don't Worry, Be Happy

Don't Worry, Be Happy needs two or more players. Players take turns telling each other what or who makes them happy. Everyone can share as many things as they can think of that create happiness in their lives, such as "My dog's kisses make me happy," "A warm day at the beach makes me happy," or "I like fried chicken and mashed potatoes; they make me happy." The game ends when everyone has had a turn to share.

What's in a Name?

What's in a Name? is played with two or more players. The power of observation is used in this game. Players take turns and make up silly (but respectful) names for other people they see, and then share why they think these are good nicknames.

Appropriate silly names could be, "His name is Long Tall Jim. He's so tall he can get cats out of trees without a ladder" or "Her name is Sweet Sue, and she makes delicious candy and cookies." This game encourages imagination but must be played with clear-cut and strictly enforced rules about respecting others.

 ## Whose Shoes?

Whose Shoes? needs at least two players. Players observe others around them and the shoes that they are wearing. Then they count and sort all the different types of shoes they see. Categories of shoes can include everything from the color of shoes, those with laces, slip-ons, sandals, boots, high heels, work boots, open-toed shoes, athletic shoes, shoes without socks, and shoes with socks. Which type is seen most? Least? What kind of shoes do most children, men, or women wear? The game ends when no player can find any more of the selected type of shoes.

CHAPTER 8

GROUP GAMES

All games in this chapter are meant to be played in groups. A group can be defined as three or more players unless otherwise specified.

 ### Will You Buy My Monkey?

Will You Buy My Monkey? needs a minimum of four players. Players sit in a circle except for a player who has been chosen (or has volunteered) to be the monkey and another player who has been chosen or has volunteered to be the monkey seller. The object of the game is for the seller to sell her monkey to the other players. She goes from player to player asking, "Will you buy my monkey?" A player must answer "No, thank you" without smiling or laughing. Then the seller says, "My monkey can do many things, like . . . " At this point, the monkey does the things the seller says it can do, such as hop on one foot, wiggle her nose, or do a ballet dance. Again, the player asked to buy the monkey says, "No, thank you," with a straight face. If the player does not smile or laugh, the seller continues to ask other players in the circle to buy the monkey. If that player laughs or smiles, he becomes the monkey, the current monkey becomes the monkey seller, and the current seller joins the circle.

 ### Drop the Handkerchief

Drop the Handkerchief is played by six or more players. One player is It. All players except It stand in a circle facing in. It walks around outside the circle (behind the other players' backs) with a handkerchief (or other unbreakable, small object) in her hand. She drops the handkerchief quietly behind a player and keeps walking, trying to get partway around the circle before the player notices the handkerchief behind him. When the player finds the handkerchief, he picks it up and runs, trying to tag It before she can get around the circle and back to his open space. If he can't tag her, he becomes It for the next round of play. If he does tag her, she continues as It for another round.

X Marks the Spot

One player is the leader of X Marks the Spot. Players stand together in a group while the leader points out a spot on the ground or floor near where the group is standing. After all players have seen the spot, they close or cover their eyes and one at a time walk slowly until they think they have reached the spot. When a player thinks she has reached the right place, she stops, opens her eyes, and stands there until all other players have had their turn. The player getting closest to the right spot, as decided by the leader, will be the leader for the next round of play.

Number Switcharoo

Number Switcharoo requires at least eight players. One player, the leader, gives each player a different number before the start of the game. All players, except for the leader, sit in a circle, while the leader stands in the middle of the circle. When play begins, the leader calls out two numbers. The players with those two numbers run and switch places before the leader can sit in one of the open spots. If the players are able to switch spots, play continues with the leader calling out additional numbers. If the leader is able to sit in one of the open spots, the player left out becomes the new leader.

See It? Do It!

In See It? Do It! all players (including the leader) stand in a circle. The leader says, "When I went to the pet store, I saw a cat do this," and then he acts out something a cat could do, such as licking a paw, chasing his tail, or purring. All other players imitate this action. Then the player to the left of the leader takes a turn, saying, "When I went to the farm, I saw a goat do this," and she makes gestures, sounds and movements of a goat. The game continues until all players have had a turn adding another animal's antics or players are laughing too hard to continue.

Balancing Act

Balancing Act needs a minimum of three players, each with a small, flat rock at least 1½ inches. One player is the leader. All players except the leader line up side by side at one end of the playing area with a rock balanced on the toe of one shoe. At the leader's "Go" signal, players walk as carefully as they can toward a designated finish line, trying to keep the rock from falling off their shoes. If the rock falls off their shoes, the player returns to the starting line and begins again. The first player to cross the finish line is the winner.

How Touching

In How Touching, players stand in a line behind a leader. The leader takes the first turn and touches an item that is visible to all players. The next player in line touches the same object and then touches an additional object. Play continues with the third player touching the first two objects and then an additional object. Each new player adds on to the chain of objects. Players must touch the objects in the correct order, or they are out of the round of play. To encourage cooperative play, players may tap another player's shoulder if they need help remembering the order in which the objects were touched. Play continues until everyone has had a turn. The player who remembered the longest series of objects gets to be the leader for the next round. If all players have the same score, the leader initiates another round of play.

A Tisket, a Tasket

In A Tisket, a Tasket, all players stand in a large circle and choose one player to be the dropper. This player leaves the circle and runs around the outside of it. Players in the circle sing the song below. When the verse ends, the dropper drops a small object, such as a beanbag or a piece of cloth, behind the back of a player standing in the circle. That player becomes the chaser. He picks up the item and tries to catch the dropper, who races around the circle, before she reaches the chaser's spot. If caught, the dropper joins the circle, and the player who caught her becomes the next dropper. If the dropper is not caught, she moves around the circle as the verse is repeated for another round of play.

Standard lyrics for the game are as follows:

A-tisket, a-tasket,

A green and yellow basket.

I wrote a letter to my friend,

And on the way I dropped it,

I dropped it, I dropped it,

And on the way I dropped it.

Another friend picked it up,

And put it in their pocket.

 ## Button, Button, Who's Got the Button?

Button, Button, Who's Got the Button? is played by six or more players. One player is the leader. All other players form a circle, cup their hands and hold them out horizontally, palms together in a praying fashion. The leader takes an object such as a button and goes around the circle, wedging her folded hands in between everybody else's hands, one by one, dropping the button into one player's hands along the way so that no one knows who received the button. When the leader has finished going around the circle, she says, "Button, button, who's got the button?" and then each player in the circle takes a turn guessing who has the button. The player guessing replies, "(Logan) has the button!" When the player with the button is guessed, the player who guessed correctly becomes the new leader, and another round of play starts. If nobody guesses correctly by the time it gets to the player with the button, he shows it to everyone and becomes the leader for the next round of play.

Variation: The leader stands in the center of the circle while the button is secretly passed behind the backs of players in the circle, stopping at random. The trick is to do this so carefully that the leader can't tell where or when the button-passing has stopped. When one player is holding the button behind his back, the leader tries to guess where the button is. When the button is found, the leader takes the place of the player in the circle who has the button. The player with the button becomes the leader, and play begins again.

 ## Tug of War

Tug of War is played by five or more players and requires a rope or other sturdy piece of cord, a small piece of cloth, and two teams with an equal number of players, preferably of like strength. Before the game begins, a circle of approximately two feet is drawn on the ground. The rope is placed across the middle of the circle, and the cloth is tied in the middle of the rope. Teams stand in single-file lines and grab the rope with both hands. One player chosen to be the leader signals "Pull," and the teams pull backward on the rope, trying to get the center cloth out of the circle and toward their side. The team that moves the cloth over the line to their side of the circle is the winner of the round of play.

Silly Sally's Cool Club

One player is the leader of Silly Sally's Cool Club. Players sit or stand in a circle with the leader in the middle. The leader explains that Silly Sally has a cool club and that they will be trying to join the club. The only way players can join is if they can figure out what Sally likes and doesn't like, by asking yes or no questions. For example, a player may ask, "Does Sally like crackers?" The secret is that Sally likes only things that have double letters in them. Sally likes soccer, but she doesn't like golf. Sally likes strawberries, but she doesn't like grapes. When a player thinks he has figured out the secret to what Sally likes, he whispers his answer to the leader. If he is right, the leader allows him in the club by having him join her in the center of the circle. Other players continue asking questions until they learn the secret, or play can end after the first player tells everyone what the secret is.

> **Variation:** The rule to get into the club can be changed according to players' abilities. Some examples of rules may include beginning sounds or rhyming words.

Who's Got the Bone?

In Who's Got the Bone? one player plays the part of the dog, and another player assumes the role of the leader. The dog sits in a chair with his back to the other players. A small object such as a rock or wad of paper is put under the dog's chair; that is the bone. The dog closes his eyes. When he does, the leader points to another player who sneaks up, takes the bone, and hides it behind her back. When the bone is hidden, all players chant, "Doggy, Doggy, who's got your bone? Someone took it from your home." Then the dog has three guesses to figure out who took it. If the dog guesses correctly, he gets another turn to be the dog. If he guesses wrong, the player who has hidden the bone gets a turn to be the dog.

The Ship's Captain

In the Ship's Captain, one player, the captain, stands facing the other players. He calls out orders to the rest of the players, who are the crew. If the captain notices a player who does not follow an order, she is out of the game for that round and moves away from the other players. This decision of who sits out is made by the captain, who is always right. The captain continues giving orders until only one crew member is left in the game. That player becomes the captain for the next round of play.

Examples of the captain's orders to his crew are:

- To the ship: All players run to the captain's right.
- To the island: All players run to the captain's left.
- Hit the deck: All players lie down on their stomachs or crouch down.
- Attention on deck: All players salute and yell, "Aye, aye

captain!" Players may not move until the captain gives the order of, "At ease!" Even if the captain gives a different order such as "To the ship," players must remain at attention until told "at ease."

- Three crew in a boat: Players form groups of two or three and sing, "Row, row, row your boat."
- The love boat: Players get a partner and dance.
- Clear the deck: Players sit down and pull their feet up off the floor.
- Scrub the deck: All players get on their knees and pretend to scrub the floor.
- Captain's quarters: Players run toward the captain.
- Man overboard: Players find a partner as quickly as possible. One partner lies on her stomach on the floor while the other partner gently puts his foot on his partner's back.
- Up periscope: All players lay on their back and stick one leg in the air.
- SHARK!: Players run to a designated home base that is known by all players before the start of the game (multiple bases can be used when the game is played by a large group).
- Sick turtle: Players lay on their back and wave hands and feet in the air.
- Row the boat: Each player finds a partner, sits face to face, holds hands, and pretends to row a boat.

Bananas

In Bananas, all players sit in a circle except the leader, who stands in the middle of the circle. One at a time, players ask the leader any question, but the only answer she can give is "Bananas." The leader needs to keep a straight face without laughing or smiling when answering the questions. For example, a player might ask, "What is your favorite color?" or "What is your pet's name?" and the answer is "Bananas." The first player to make the leader laugh or smile gets a turn to be the leader for the next round.

Seven Up, Stand Up

Seven Up, Stand Up needs a minimum of fourteen players. Up to seven players are chosen as It and stand together as a group in front of other players as the game begins. All other players sit in a circle and cover their eyes with one hand or put their heads down in their laps. They hold up a fist with their thumb up in the air. At the start of the game, while the other players are not looking, the seven players who are It move silently around, each selecting a player and pushing down that person's thumb. When the seven It players have pushed down a thumb, they return to the front of the group and say, "Seven up, stand up." At this time, all players open their eyes. The players whose thumbs were tapped stand up and have one guess at who touched their thumb. If they guess correctly, they exchange places and become an It. If they are incorrect, the player who pushed their thumb down continues to be an It for the next round of play.

> **Variations:** If the game is played with a small group, only two or three players (instead of seven) can be chosen as It.

Ruffle Your Feathers

In Ruffle Your Feathers, all players but one, the leader, stand in a circle. The leader stands in the middle. The players forming the circle start to flap their arms like a bird. Then the leader names different types of animals, claiming they have feathers (whether or not they actually do). For example, the leader may say, "Birds have feathers," "Bats have feathers," or "Butterflies have feathers." Each time the leader names an animal, depending on whether or not the animal actually does have feathers, the players either flap their arms or don't. If players flap their arms when the animal doesn't have feathers or don't flap their arms when the animal does have feathers, they must sit down. The leader can flap his wings on any animal, trying to confuse the other players, and calls out animals as rapidly as possible. The last player standing in the circle is the leader for the next round of play.

Blind Chicken

Blind Chicken is played by five or more players in an open area without tripping hazards or furniture, and the boundaries are identified to all players before the game starts. One player is It, and another player is the leader. The player who is It is the blind chicken and blindfolded. At the leader's "Go" signal, all other players move quietly around the blind chicken, trying to keep from being caught. If the blind chicken tags a player by touching or grabbing her, he tries to recognize the player by touch. The blind chicken has two guesses to figure out who the player is. If he fails, she is let go and the game continues. If the blind chicken guesses correctly, the tagged player becomes the next blind chicken.

Fruits and Veggies

In Fruits and Veggies, one player is the leader, and other players divide into two groups. The leader gives each player in one group the name of a vegetable, and the other group a fruit. In each group, at least two players have the same name. For example, two players in the fruit group are apples, and two players in the vegetable group are broccoli. Then the leader closes his eyes and counts to ten while all players mix themselves up and sit in a large circle. After all players are seated, the leader sits in the middle of the circle. The leader then gives instructions to the other players, such as "Peas and apples change places." While the players are moving, the leader tries to steal a free place. If he succeeds, the player left without a place to sit becomes the new leader for the next round of play.

Follow the Leader

In Follow the Leader, one player is the guesser. The other players sit in a circle while the guesser stands temporarily outside the circle or covers her eyes so she cannot see the other players while they choose a secret leader. Then the guesser returns to the middle of the circle or opens her eyes to watch the group. The secret leader starts a motion that all other players will copy. For example, the leader may wink, and everyone must wink. The leader can change motions from time to time, and the other players copy this gesture. The guesser has three guesses to find the secret leader. If she guesses correctly, the leader becomes the guesser. If she does not guess correctly, the secret leader chooses another player to be guesser, and the game continues with the same rules for the next round of play.

 ## Yum or Yuck

The singing game Yum or Yuck is played to the tune of "Alouetta." One player is the leader. All other players stand in a circle and sing the following, while the leader stands in the middle:

Group: Peanut butter, we like peanut butter.

Peanut butter, that's the stuff for us.

Do you like peanut butter on your tongue? (Players point to

the leader.)

*Leader: I like peanut butter on my tongue. (*The leader sticks

out his tongue while saying this.)

Or I like peanut butter on my toes (nose or arms). (The leader

points to the named body part.)

Group: On your tongue? Or on your toes (nose or arms)? (All

players copy the gesture done by the leader.)

Leader: Yes, I do. Yes, I do.

All: Oh, oh, oh, oh, oh.

Play continues with the leader choosing another leader for the next round of play.

> **Variations:** Change peanut butter to another food such as spaghetti, mac and cheese, or fried chicken. Or for a really silly version, use items that no one likes to eat, such as slimy worms, stinky fish, or broccoli ice cream.

Motor Boat

Motor Boat is played by a minimum of two players, who hold hands and form a circle. They walk in the same direction while they chant the following verse:

Motor boat, motor boat, go so slow.

Motor boat, motor boat, go so fast.

Motor boat, motor boat, step on the gas.

Vroooommmmm!

Motor boat, motor boat, go so slow.

Chug, chug.

Motor boat, motor boat, out of gas.

Players walk faster as they recite the verse through Vroooom-mmmm! and then gradually slow down. At the last line, players come to a stop and sit on the ground.

Who Stole the Cookie?

Who Stole the Cookie? needs a minimum of three players. One player is the leader. All players sit together in a circle with their legs crossed, and the leader starts each part of the chant. During the entire chant, all players, including the leader, continue to slap their thighs once, then clap hands once in a rhythmic pattern. The faster the chant, the more challenging the game.

Leader: Who stole the cookie from the cookie jar?

Group: Who stole the cookie from the cookie jar?

Leader: (First name of a player) stole the cookie from the cookie jar.

Group: (First name of a player) stole the cookie from the cookie jar.

Named player: Not me.

Group: Yes, you.

Named player: Couldn't be.

Group: Then who?

Named player: (Name of another player) stole the cookie from
the cookie jar.

Group: (Name of another player) stole the cookie from the cookie
jar.

The chant is repeated until all players have been named for stealing a cookie from the cookie jar.

Red Rover, Red Rover

Red Rover, Red Rover needs at least eight players, divided into two teams. Players on each team hold hands and line up side by side at either end of a playing area with the two teams facing each other. One team goes first, and while walking toward the other team says, "Red Rover, Red Rover, send (a player's name from the other team) right over." The player whose name was called runs as fast as she can toward the opposing side and tries to run through and break the grip of two players who are holding hands. If she does not break through, she joins the opposing team, but if she does, she can take one of the two players whose link she broke back to her team. Teams take turns calling to Red Rover until one team is left with only one player.

> **Note:** To ensure the safety of all players, close supervision by an adult is needed. Players need to be reminded of the correct way to break the hand link of two players (only at the wrists of players). Players not following this rule must be removed from the game.

Lemonade

Players divide into two teams for Lemonade. Team A players are the actors while Team B players are the guessers. Each team needs to choose a home base to run to for safety and stay there until the beginning of the game. All actors decide on an action familiar to everyone to act out as a group, such as climbing a tree or driving a car, without letting the guessers know what they have chosen. The game begins with all players walking from their respective home base toward the center of the playing area while saying the following:

A: *Here we come.*

B: *Where are you from?*

A: *New Orleans.*

B: *What's your trade?*

A: *Lemonade.*

B: *Show us something, if you're not afraid.*

At this point, actors stop walking and start their chosen action. Team B has three tries to guess what the action is. If the guessers are right, actors must run to their base without being tagged by a guesser. If all three guesses are wrong, guessers must run to their base without being tagged by an actor. Any player tagged must switch teams. The game is over when all players are caught and on the same team.

 ## The Loose Caboose

In the Loose Caboose, one player is selected to be the loose caboose, and the rest of the players are grouped into trains of three. It's okay if a train has one more or less player. Players create their train by holding onto the waist of the player in front of them. The first player in a train is the engine. As the game begins, the loose caboose and the trains chug (shuffle their feet) around the playing area with appropriate train sound effects. The object is for the loose caboose to attach to the end of any train. The engine on each team tries to steer his train away from the loose caboose. When the caboose attaches to the back of a train, the engine of that train becomes the new loose caboose.

Mouse Trap

For Mouse Trap, one player is the leader, and the other players divide into two groups. Uneven teams are okay. One group is the trap, and the other is made of the mice. The trap group forms a circle by standing and holding hands in the air. The mice run around the playing area, weaving in and out of the trap. The leader stands with her back to the trap and says, "Mouse trap." At this signal, the trap players lower their arms. Any mouse inside the trap is caught and becomes part of the trap. The last free mouse is the winner and becomes the leader for the next round of play.

 ## Toe Tapping

One player is chosen to be the leader. The other players are divided into pairs. Each pair sits facing each other, holding hands. At the leader's signal, "Go", players try to tap the tops of each other's toes using their own toes. When one of the partners scores three taps, the pair lie on the ground until the other pairs are successful. Once everyone has completed the toe tapping, it's time to choose a new leader and switch partners.

> Variation: Partners lie on the floor, feet to feet or big toe to big toe and at the "Go" signal, roll across the floor, keeping their toes or feet touching at all times.

 ## I'm the Hokey Pokey

I'm the Hokey Pokey is much like the classic Hokey Pokey action song (see page 146) with one player featured in the spotlight. All players stand in a circle and choose one player to be in the center (in the spotlight). The group sings the spotlighted player's name, and he acts out the song's directions. Players in the circle join in the actions done by the spotlight player during the chorus. The song may sound like this: "We put Nathan in, we take Nathan out, we put Nathan in, and he shakes it all about." Then all players sing and act out the chorus.

> Variation: To include more players at one time, all players with certain features such as brown hair, tied shoes, or blue eyes are in the spotlight.

Silent Signals

Before beginning Silent Signals, players invent and practice three hand signals or gestures that represent three categories: animals, colors, and people's names. For example, the gesture for animal might be one finger spun around in a circle, color might be clapping hands, and a person's name might be winking or blinking eyes. The more alike the motions are, the more difficult the game. One player, the leader, points to any player and calls out words that fit into one of the three categories. She might call out words such as "giraffe," "purple," or "Malcolm." The player pointed to has to give the correct hand signal for each word. Players receive one point for each correct hand signal. Play continues until everyone has had a turn to give the hand signals; then it's another player's turn to be the leader. After three rounds, the player with the highest score wins.

Squeeze Hide and Go Seek

In Squeeze Hide and Go Seek, one player takes off to find a hiding place large enough for all players, while everyone else counts slowly to fifty. After reaching fifty, a second player goes to find the first, while a third player from the group counts to fifty. When the second player finds the first, she joins him in the hiding place. If she cannot find the player, she returns to the group and is out of the game. Next, the third player goes to find the hiding spot while a fourth player counts to fifty. The game continues until all players have had a turn to find everyone.

Islands

Full newspaper pages, or a similar size of paper, and music (recorded or sung) are needed for Islands. The pages are the islands, which are put on the ground around the room (one for each player) minus the leader, who controls the music. The goal of the game is to stand on an island without falling off. The game begins with all players except the leader standing on an island. As music is played, players walk while making swimming motions and move from island to island until the music stops. When the music stops, everyone races to get on an island. When everyone is on an island, the music begins again, the players start swimming, and the leader removes one of the islands. As before, when the music stops, players race to stand on an island. As islands are removed, it becomes more challenging for players to stand together without falling off. Players can help each other stay on an island; if one islander falls off, the entire group on that island is out of the game. Islands are removed until only one is left. The winner is the last group of players who can all stand on an island without falling off.

The Bear Went Over the Mountain

The Bear Went Over the Mountain is best played in a large indoor or outdoor playing area and needs at least three players, one of whom is the leader. All players are bears who follow and copy the actions of the leader, which are based on the chant that everyone sings. The leader's actions change with each verse of the chant to illustrate the movement such as "over the mountain," "around the mountain," or "through the mountain."

The bear went _____ the mountain.

The bear went _____ the mountain.

The bear went _____ the mountain.

To see what he (or she) could see.

After the players have sung the verse, they take turns telling what the bear saw. For instance, players could guess the bear saw a big mountain made of ice cream or a flock of pink and purple polka-dotted birds. Silly answers to what the bear saw make the game more fun.

> Variations: Two players hold hands together over their heads to represent the mountain while the other players complete the actions according to the verses. For example, players go through their arch when the verse "The bear went through the mountain" is sung. After the last line, players take turns telling what the bear saw.

 ## Mother (or Father) May I?

Mother May I? needs a minimum of three players. One player is the mother (or father). The other players stand side by side in a line at one end of the playing area, facing the mother. She takes turns calling to each player, telling him what kind of movement he can do to move forward or backward from the starting line. For instance, "Derrick, you may take two baby steps forward." Players called must ask, "Mother, may I?" before moving according to what the mother said. She either replies "Yes, you may" or "No, you may not, but you may _____ instead" and inserts another suggestion. The players usually move closer to the mother but are sometimes led farther away. Even if the mother makes an unfavorable suggestion, the player must perform it. Players can move only with mother's permission when it's their turn or without the mother's permission when it's not their turn, but if mother sees them doing so, she sends them back to the starting line.

Movements may include the following steps:

- Take (#) steps forward.
- Take (#) giant steps forward or backward (usually a small number, due to large step size).
- Take (#) baby steps forward or backward (usually a large number, due to tiny step size).
- Take (#) umbrella steps forward (twirling around while moving forward).
- Hop forward like a frog, (#) times.
- Run forward for (#) seconds.

- Crabwalk forward for (#) seconds (done with hands on the ground behind and legs straight out front).
- Take (#) Cinderella steps (twirl forward with an index finger touching the top of the head).
- Open and shut the book (#) times (jump forward with feet apart then again bringing the feet together).
- Take (#) scissor steps forward (long strides with each leg swung directly in front of the other).
- Run backward for (#) seconds.
- Walk backward until I say "stop."
- Return to the starting line.

When a player is close enough to tag mother, he becomes the new mother (or father) and the game begins again.

> Variations: To make the game easier, the mother calls out only one or two different types of steps and eliminates the "Mother, may I?" response, so no player is sent back to the starting place. To make the game more challenging, players can make up their own steps, such as dancers' leaps or twirls, football kicks, air guitar, or other dance steps.

 ## Elves, Giants, Wizards

Elves, Giants, Wizards is based on the game Rock, Paper, Scissors (see pages 158–159). Players split into two competing teams. Each team has a home base to run to at the end of each round. At the beginning of each round, each team secretly chooses to be elves, giants, or wizards. To begin, the two teams stand face to face in parallel lines about six feet apart in the middle of the playing area. Both groups yell, "Elves, giants, wizards." Then each member of the team gives the action appropriate for their team's choice:

- Elves: Players squat low to the ground and put a finger on either side of their heads like pointed ears.
- Giants: Players stand on tiptoe and stretch arms high over their head.

- Wizards: Players turn their bodies ninety degrees to the left, stretch their right arms out in front, put their left hand by their left shoulder, and wiggle their fingers like they are casting a spell.

Elves beat wizards (because they can run through their legs). Giants beat elves (because they are taller and stronger). Wizards beat giants (because they are smarter). The winners then chase the other team's players back to their home base and try to tag them. Players tagged join the other team. The game is over when everyone is on one team.

Abba Jabba

Players in Abba Jabba need to have enough room to move without bumping into each other. At the beginning of the game, players have one hand on their stomach and their other hand on their head. One player, the leader, says, "One, two, three, go," at which time all players move their stomach hand in a circular motion in a counterclockwise direction and use their other hand to pat their head. A simpler patting motion with both hands is acceptable if this is too difficult for some players. While they are doing this, players repeat, "Abba, jabba, abba, jabba." Players who lose the rhythm or end up laughing must sit down and wait for the game to end. The last player to remain standing is the winner and the new leader for the next round of play.

> Note: This game really gets the wiggles out. Players are exhausted when the game is over.

Alphabet Switcharoo

In Alphabet Switcheroo, all players need a designated place to stand that is marked, so other players know each other's places. This can be done by players drawing a circle around their feet with chalk or tape, having a beanbag, small rock, or twig where they stand, or some other method. Players stand in a large circle about six feet from each other, with one player, the leader, standing in the middle. When all players are ready, the leader calls out a letter, such as O. All players with an O in their name have to change places with someone else in the circle. At the same time, the leader runs around trying to take an open spot. The player left without a place becomes the leader, and the play continues. The leader can also say, "Alphabet switcheroo," at which time all players change places and hope not to be left without a base and thus be the leader for the next round of play.

Corners

Corners is played by five players in an area that has four corners or spots designated as corners, such as a tree, chair, or bush. One player is the leader and stands in the middle of the playing area while each of the four other players stand in one of the corners. When the leader says "Change," everyone runs from one corner to another corner at the same time that the leader is trying to steal a corner spot. If the leader gets to a corner, the player who loses her corner takes a turn at being the leader.

Cooperation Relay

In Cooperation Relay, one person is the leader. The game requires two balls, such as soccer balls, one for each team. Within each team, players divide into partners (if there is an uneven number of players, one team member may have two partners). Each team lines up in pairs behind a starting line. On the leader's "Go" signal, the first pair on each team together carries a ball (approximately the size of a soccer ball) to a designated spot and back to the next pair, without using their hands. If the ball is dropped, it must be repositioned, and the pair continues from that place rather than starting over. Partners may carry their ball in their own way such as between their knees, heads, stomachs, elbows, or another way, just without using their hands. The game is over when all players on one team have successfully carried the ball to and from the starting line.

Air Ball

All players stand in a circle and number off, starting with one before Air Ball begins. One player stands in the middle of the circle and throws a ball up as high as he can while calling out a number. The player given that number tries to catch the ball before it hits the ground. If she is successful, she moves into the center of the circle, throws the ball as high as possible, and calls out another number. If the ball touches the ground, the last player who threw it gets another turn. This is a cooperative game, as the goal is to get as many consecutive catches as possible. Play continues until all players have had their numbers called.

Wall Ball

Wall Ball needs a small ball about the size of a tennis ball, a wall without windows or furniture close by, and an open playing area. The goal is for a player to throw the ball at the wall and then quickly perform certain actions, in order. Players take turns. If a player misses, he has to start over from the beginning of the list on his next turn. The first player to complete all eight actions is the winner.

Actions, in order of difficulty, that can be used in Wall Ball:

1. Throw the ball and catch it before it bounces on the ground.
2. Throw the ball and catch it after one bounce on the ground.
3. Throw the ball and catch it after two bounces on the ground.
4. Throw the ball and catch it after you touch your hands to the ground once.
5. Throw the ball and clap your hands before you catch it.
6. Throw the ball and touch your knees before you catch it.
7. Lift one leg, throw the ball under your knee and then catch it.
8. Throw the ball and turn in a circle before you catch it.

> Variation: To make the game more challenging, complete the actions using a nondominant hand.

Wheelbarrow

Wheelbarrow is done in pairs but also needs a leader. The game is safest when players are matched in size and physical strength and it is played in an area free of tripping hazards. All pairs line up at one end of the playing area, and a finish line is noted. One player puts both her hands on the floor/ground while the other player stands between her legs and picks up both her ankles. The leader gives a "Go" signal, and the pairs race in this position to the finish line. The distance between start and finish should be set according to the abilities of the players. The first pair to complete the race is the winner.

> Variation: For more physically developed players, an obstacle course may present additional challenges.

Roll Out the Barrel

Roll Out the Barrel is played in pairs but also needs a leader. The game is safest when players are matched in size and physical strength and it is played in an area free of tripping hazards. Players put their arms over their head and join hands with their partner with their fingers locked together. The leader gives a "Go" signal, and the pair twist around and walk in the same direction while continuing to keep their hands connected. A start and finish line can be added if players want to race, but to keep players safe without competing, there should be only one pair of players rolling out their barrel at any time.

Leap Frog

Leap Frog is played in pairs and needs a leader. The game is safest when players are matched in size and physical strength and it is played in an area free of tripping hazards, with players spaced so that they don't run into each other. Each pair has a frog and a lily pad. The frogs stand behind the lily pads, who are squatting very low on the ground. The leader gives a "Go" signal, and then all frogs place their hands on the backs of the lily pads, legs apart, and leap over their partner. After a frog has leapt over a lily pad, he squats down on the ground, becoming the lily pad, and his partner stands up, becoming the new frog. The new frog jumps over the lily pad, and play continues with the partners switching roles and moving in a straight line. A start and finish line can be added to create a team race, or this game can just be played to promote cooperation.

9 HOLIDAY GAMES

New Year's Eve Games

New Year's Eve Charades

New Year's Eve Charades needs a minimum of four players. They divide into two teams, preferably of equal size, but if it is not possible, one player will have an extra turn. A player from each team is the timekeeper. Before the start of the game, each player writes a New Year's resolution on a slip of paper, folds it, and places it in a container. Then a player from Team A draws a resolution slip from the container. It is her job to act out the resolution for her teammates. After she reads it, the timekeeper for Team B notes the time and tells the player to start. Then Team A has three minutes to guess the resolution. If Team A figures it out, the timekeeper records how long it took. If Team A does not figure it out in three minutes, the timekeeper states that time is up and records a time of three minutes. Then a player from Team B draws a slip, and play proceeds. The game continues until every player has had a chance to act out a resolution. The score for each team is the total time that the team needed for all of the rounds. The team with the smallest score wins the game.

Valentine's Day Games

The Queen (or King) of Hearts

The Queen of Hearts needs at least six players. One player is the king of hearts, and one player is the queen of hearts.

These two players sit on a chair in front of the other players. One player is the knave. All other players are guests of the queen or king of hearts and stand forming a circle. Each person's designated spot is marked by a beanbag, small flat counter, or small piece of paper. Whenever the queen or king calls out "Change places," the players race to a new spot while the knave tries to "steal a spot" to stand on. Whoever has no spot to stand on is the new knave, and the game continues.

> Note: It may be necessary to explain that a *knave* is a storybook character who tries to take things away from others.

Cupid Says

Cupid Says is played with the same rules as Simon Says (page 55), with Cupid giving the commands. Players follow his directions only if he begins his commands with "Cupid says." If Cupid does not begin his commands this way, players do not obey. Any player who does not follow the rules correctly is out of the game. The last player to remain in the game is the winner and becomes the new Cupid.

Presidents' Day Games

Pitching Pennies

Pitching Pennies needs at least two players, a shallow container or dish, and plenty of pennies. The empty container is placed on the floor while all players sit or stand behind a starting line (a longer distance for more skillful players). Players take turns trying to toss pennies into the open container "heads up" (so Lincoln's head is visible). To make this a competitive game, players keep track of the number of pennies they toss into the container, with the winner having the most pennies heads up inside it. Or, the game can be played in a noncompetitive way to promote skill development and cooperative fun.

> Variation: To make the game more challenging, players try to get the pennies into the container using only two fingers or can flick a penny by using the edge of another penny to get it in.

St. Patrick's Day Games

The Leprechaun Says

The Leprechaun Says is played with the same rules as Simon Says (page 55), with the leprechaun giving the commands. Players follow his directions only if he begins his commands with "The Leprechaun says." If the leprechaun does not begin his commands this way, players do not obey. Any player who does not follow the rules correctly is out of the game. The last player to remain in the game is the winner and becomes the new leprechaun.

A Leprechaun's Bag of Tricks

A Leprechaun's Bag of Tricks needs at least five players. One player is the leader. This game takes players into the make-believe world of leprechauns and their magic bags. Before the game starts, three or four small objects, such as a pencil, key, or paper clip, are put into a small bag by the leader. Then all other players divide into two teams; it's okay if one team has one more or less player. If playing with only a few players, players are paired together. One team has the bag with the items. Without showing the other team what is in the bag, the team uses the objects in the bag to make up a story and act it out. The name of each object in the bag must be mentioned at least twice in the story. After the story is finished, the players on the other team try to guess all the objects in the leprechaun's bag. Then the leader puts three or four different objects in the bag for the next team to have a turn to tell and act out a story.

April Fool's Day Games

All Mixed Up

All Mixed Up is for a minimum of three players. Before the game begins, players take off their shoes and put them in a pile in the middle of the playing area, near where the leader stands. All other players stand or sit behind a starting line at one end of the area. At the leader's "Go" signal, players run to the shoe pile to find their own shoes but put them on the wrong feet and then run back to the starting line. The first player to get back to the starting line is the winner.

> **Variation:** For added April Fool's Day fun, players can play games, such as Simple Tag or musical chairs, while wearing their shoes on the wrong feet.

Spring Games

They're Good Eggs

Egg games or egg hunts are traditional American events each spring. Although there are many more, the three here are easy to adapt for players of any age or ability.

1. Each player is given a plastic or hard-boiled egg, except the player who is the leader. Players get down on their hands and knees and line up behind the starting line with their noses on their egg. The leader stands to one side of the other players and gives a "Go" signal for players to push their egg with their noses only to the finish line.

2. Players divide into two teams and stand in a line behind a starting line, except the player who is the leader. If one team has one fewer player, one player will have an extra turn. Each team is given a spoon (larger ones are best for younger players) and a plastic or hard-boiled egg. The leader stands to one side of the other players and gives the "Go" signal. The first player in line races to the finish line and back again with her egg

balanced in the spoon. If it drops, she must pick it up and return to the starting line to try again. Each player in turn runs with the egg in a spoon from and back to the starting line. The winner is the team to finish first.

3. This game is played in stocking feet and with a plastic egg. Players take turns trying to get their eggs through a goal post without the egg becoming airborne (two chairs two feet apart work well as a goal post). For more skilled players, the distance to the goal post or span of the goal post should be adjusted to make the game more challenging. Score can be kept, or all players can celebrate when a goal is made.

Laughing Eggs

Laughing Eggs is played by a minimum of five players in an area with a noted safe zone at the far end. One player is the fox, and another is the hen. All other players are eggs. The hen chooses a color for each egg by whispering it in each player's ear. At the beginning of the game, the eggs line up facing the hen. The fox comes up behind the hen and pretends he is knocking on her door.

Hen: Who is it?

Fox: It's the fox.

Hen: What do you want?

Fox: Your eggs.

Hen: I don't have any.

Eggs: (Loud laughter)

Fox: I hear them laughing.

Hen: Okay, what color do you want?

The fox calls out a color, at which time, those eggs run to the opposite side of the playing area to the safe zone. If the fox catches an egg, a new fox and a new hen are picked. If the fox doesn't catch any eggs before they make it to the safe zone, he guesses another color, trying to catch a laughing egg. The fox always knocks on the door and repeats the conversation between him and the hen before he can ask for eggs of a new color.

May Day Games

Flower Basket Upset

Flower Basket Upset is for ten or more players. One player is the leader and assigns the name of a flower to each of the other players. At least three players should have the same flower name. Before the game begins, all players except the leader sit in a circle (either in chairs or on the ground) during the game. When the game begins, the leader stands in the middle of the circle and calls out any flower or combination of flowers. Players with that flower name must get up and switch chairs, while the leader tries to sit in one of their chairs. The leader can choose to call out "Flower basket upset," and at that time, all players get up and switch chairs. The player not finding a chair to sit in is the leader for the next round of play.

Flag Day Games

Capture the Flag

Capture the Flag is for six or more players. One player is the leader and stands to one side of a large, open playing area. Other players are divided into two equal teams if possible, but it's okay if teams are uneven. A red flag is given to a player on one team, and a blue flag is given to a player on the other team. Each team selects a home base in the playing area, and uses that base to hide the flag. At the leader's "Go" signal, teams try to capture the other team's flag and bring it back to their home base to win. If a player is tagged by an opposing team member, she moves outside the playing area, sometimes called a jail. Players

> Note: Out of respect, our American flag should not be used when playing this game.

can get out of jail only if a player from their team tags them. The game is over when the flag from an opposing team is captured and taken home.

Fourth of July Games

Uncle Sam Says

Uncle Sam Says has the same rules as Simon Says (page 55), except Uncle Sam is giving the commands now. Players follow his directions only if he begins his commands with "Uncle Sam says." If Uncle Sam does not begin his commands this way, players do not obey. Any player who does not follow the directions correctly is out of the game. The last player to remain in the game is the winner and becomes the new Uncle Sam.

Uncle Sam

Uncle Sam is played by a minimum of four players. All players except one, who is Uncle Sam, line up in a long line on one side of the playing area. Uncle Sam stands in the middle of the playing area while players call out, "Uncle Sam, Uncle Sam, may we cross your river dam?" Uncle Sam answers, "Yes you may, yes you may, if you're wearing (color) today!" Players wearing the color that was called out try to get to the other side of the playing area without being tagged by Uncle Sam. If they get caught, they become taggers and help Uncle Sam catch the others when he calls new colors. The winner is the last player to be tagged, and she becomes the new Uncle Sam.

Yankee Doodle Ate a Cracker

Yankee Doodle Ate a Cracker needs at least seven players and crackers. One player is Yankee Doodle. The other players are divided up into equal teams if possible; if not, a player on the team with fewer players will have two turns. Yankee Doodle passes out crackers to all players. At his "Go" signal, the first player on each team eats her cracker and tries to whistle or sing "Yankee Doodle Went to Town." As soon as she has succeeded, the next player does the same. The first team to finish wins.

Halloween Games

Ghost in the Graveyard

Ghost in the Graveyard is played by a minimum of three players in an open area. A home base is known by all players before the game begins. One player is the ghost. At the start of the game, the ghost stands at home base and calls out "one o'clock," "two o'clock," "three o'clock" and keeps going until he gets to "twelve o'clock." While the ghost is counting, all other players hide. After the ghost reaches twelve o'clock, he yells out "It's midnight," and all hiders try to run to the base before the ghost catches them. If a player is tagged, he is out of the game and becomes a spectator for the next round of play. The last player tagged becomes the ghost for the next game or round of play.

> Variation: One player is the ghost, while other players are ghost seekers. At the start of the game, ghost seekers stand together in a large open playing area and count "one o'clock, two o'clock, three o'clock, rock" (after every third number they say "rock"). When they get to midnight, all ghost seekers try to find the ghost, who has hidden somewhere in the playing area. Whoever finds the ghost yells, "Ghost in the graveyard," and all seekers run back to the home base. Whoever is first tagged by the ghost will be the next ghost.

Which Witch Are You?

Which Witch Are You? needs at least four players. One player is It. All other players sit together and are laughing witches. It sits with her eyes closed or hands covering her eyes. The witches take turns creeping close to It and laugh, disguising their voices to fool her. She tries to figure out who the laughing witch is, and if she guesses correctly, changes places with that witch and the game starts again.

Variations: The witches make spooky sounds instead of laughing, or the witches can be owls who hoot or goblins who giggle.

The Hokey Spooky

The Hokey Spooky (similar to the Hokey Pokey, page 146) needs a minimum of two players. All players stand in a circle and follow the directions as they sing:

> *You put your right hand in, you take your right hand out.*
>
> *You put your right hand in and shake it all about.*
>
> *You do the Hokey Spooky and everybody shouts.* (Players turn
>
> around with hands in the air.)
>
> *That's what it's all about. Boo!* (Players slap their thighs three
>
> times, clap hands twice, and raise hands above their heads.)

As each line is sung, the appropriate actions are done by all the players. Then the song is repeated and actions change to other body parts, such as arm, leg, elbow, hip, knee, hand, and finally whole self.

Variation: Substitute "Do the Hokey Spooky and hoot like an owl. That's what it's all about. 'Hoot!'"

Thanksgiving Games

The Thanksgiving Turkey Chase

The Thanksgiving Turkey Chase is played by at least six players with two different colors or sizes of ball; the first one is the turkey and the second one is the farmer. One player is the leader. All other players sit in a circle. At the leader's signal of "Run turkey, run!" the first ball is passed around the circle in a clockwise direction as quickly as possible. Then at the "Go, farmer, go!" signal, the second ball is passed around the circle in a counterclockwise direction. The object of the game is for players to pass the second ball around so it catches up with the first one. When this happens, the turkey gets caught. When the turkey is caught, a new leader is chosen and a new game begins.

Pilgrim, Pilgrim, Where's Your Hat?

Pilgrim, Pilgrim, Where's Your Hat? needs at least five players and a hat. One player is the Pilgrim. All other players stand or sit in a circle. The Pilgrim is blindfolded and stands in the middle of the circle. Next, the other players pass a hat to each other saying:

> *Pilgrim, pilgrim, where's your hat?*
>
> *We've passed it around the circle.*
>
> *Now, try to get it back.*

Players stop passing the hat when they have finished the verse, and the player with the hat puts it behind her back. The Pilgrim takes off his blindfold and has three tries to guess who has the hat. If he's successful, that player becomes the next Pilgrim, is blindfolded, and the game continues. If the Pilgrim does not guess correctly, he remains in the circle and the game continues.

Christmas Games

Gift Charades

Gift Charades is played by a minimum of three players. One player stands in front of the others and pantomimes a gift she received (or wants) for Christmas. The other players try to guess what the gift is. The first player to guess correctly can have the next turn to act out a gift or can choose another player who would like to act out a gift.

Hanukkah Games

Pushing Latkes

Pushing Latkes needs at least three players; beanbags, coins, or circular discs to serve as latkes (potato pancakes); and a box turned upside down with an opening cut on one side or a strip of tape taped on a table (the box or the tape represent the oven). Players stand behind a throwing line and take turns pushing their latkes into the oven by sliding their discs into the open end of the box or onto the tape strip. For each latke that goes into the oven, a player gets one point. The winner is the first player to get five points.

CHAPTER 10

PAPER AND PENCIL GAMES

All games in this chapter are meant to be played in groups. A group can be defined as three or more players unless otherwise specified.

All about You

All about You needs a minimum of two players. One player is the questioner. Players write the numbers 1 through 10 on the left side of their paper and answer the questioner's first set of ten questions without letting any other player see them.

1. Where do you wish you were right now?
2. What is your favorite color?
3. Name your favorite storybook character.
4. Write a number from 1 to 100.
5. What is the name of your pet? If you don't have one, what's the name you would give a pet?
6. Name a place in the solar system.
7. Write a number from 50 to 500.
8. What food tastes the worst to you?
9. What is your favorite zoo animal?
10. If you could play any game, what would you play? Start your answer with "Play . . ."

After all players have written their answers, the questioner reads the following questions, and players take turns reading the answers to the first set of questions. What they read won't match the first ten questions but are sure to bring smiles and chuckles to everyone.

1. Where were you born?
2. What is the color of your hair?
3. What is your favorite friend's name?
4. How old are you?
5. What is your nickname?
6. Where would you like to travel to?
7. How many people in your family?
8. What would you like to eat for dessert?
9. What would you like to get for a present?
10. What will you do in the future?

Fill the Square

Fill the Square is played by at least two players. To start the game, draw a grid with squares about one to two inches in size with a minimum of five rows and columns. The number of squares depends on the abilities of the players (having more squares makes the game more challenging, and having fewer squares simplifies the game). On the top row of the grid, write at least four categories familiar to all players, such as "Friends," "Animals," or "Colors," one category per square. It's okay if there are squares left without any words. Then players agree on a word and write one letter in each square going down the left column. For example, a player can write S-A-R-A-H with each letter in a square. When the grid is finished, players take turns choosing a square on the board and writing a word in the square that fits the category for that column and starts with the letter in that row. For instance, in the category Friends next to the letter S, a player could write Sam, and in the category Animals she could write snake. If a player cannot think of a word to add, he says, "Pass," and the next player has a turn to add a word in a square. Each player gets one point for every word written in a square. The player with the most points at the end of the game is the winner.

	Friends	Animals	Colors	
S				
A				
R				
A				
H				

Sim

Sim needs at least two players, each with a different colored pencil, marker, or crayon, and one additional color for the grid. Before the game begins, the grid is drawn: six dots form the outline of a hexagon large enough to cover a sheet of paper. Then each dot needs to be connected to every other dot by a line (see diagram below). It's important that the color of the writing utensil used to draw the dots and hexagon be of a color different from that will be used by any player.

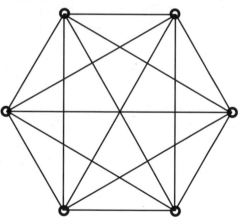

Players take turns tracing over a line between dots, trying *not* to make a triangle in their own color. The first player to complete a triangle in their own color is out, or in the case of two players, loses the game.

Cross Out

Cross Out is played by a minimum of two players, each with a sheet of paper and writing utensil. One player selects a category, such as flowers, animals, or colors. Then all players write three words on their paper in the chosen category without letting the other players see their words. Then players take turns choosing three letters they think are in other players' words. If any of the letters guessed are in opponents' words, they cross them out wherever they appear. For example, if a player's list of flowers includes *rose*, *daisy*, and *petunia*, and an opponent guesses *e*, *s*, and *a*, the player's word list would look like this: ro~~se~~, d~~a~~~~i~~~~s~~y, and p~~e~~tuni~~a~~. When all the letters in player's list are crossed out, he is out of the game. The winner is the last player left with letters not crossed out.

Shoot the Ships

Shoot the Ships requires two players. This is a simple version of the popular game Battleship. Each player needs two sheets of paper and draws one-inch squares to cover both papers. Each square in the top row is labeled by writing a number starting with one (usually going to eight), and the first column is labeled with letters down the side starting with A (usually going to M). This helps players identify squares easily, such as B6 or J2. Players use one grid to secretly place three or four ships, one ship per square, and mark these by placing an X in the selected square. The other grid is used for recording shots against his opponent's ships. Grids should be titled as "My Ships" and "(Opponent's) Ships." Players take turns trying to locate their opponent's ships by asking, "Is one of your ships in D7?" The opponent answers whether or not that square has a ship or if it's a miss. Then the asking player writes *H* on the square if a ship was hit and *M* if it was a miss. If a player gets a hit, she continues shooting until she gets a miss. The first player to sink all of his opponent's ships wins the game.

Hangman for Beginners

Hangman for Beginners is for two players who do not have reading or writing skills. One player thinks of a word, something familiar to both players. The other player asks questions about this word that can be answered with a yes or no. For example, if *boat* is the chosen word, the opponent could ask, "Is it an animal?" with the answer being no. Each time the player gets a no answer, a part of a hangman figure is drawn on a sheet of paper, such as a leg, arm, foot, body, head, or hand. The player tries to guess the word before the figure is completed.

Dots and Squares

Dots and Squares needs a minimum of two players. Before the game begins, a grid of dots, each separated by at least a half inch, is drawn on a sheet of paper. Players take turns drawing a horizontal or vertical line to connect any two dots that are next to each other. As the lines are drawn, small squares are created on the board. If a player draws the last line to complete a square, then she puts her initials inside the square and gets another turn. After the board is full of lines, the player with the most squares with his initials is the winner.

Why? Because!

Why? Because! is played by at least two players who have both reading and spelling abilities, each with a sheet of paper. On the top, each player secretly writes down a question beginning with "Why," for example, "Why do people laugh?" Then players fold their paper down just enough so the question is out of sight of other players while still leaving room to write on the paper. Players then pass their papers to a player on the right who, without looking at the question, writes an answer starting with "Because." For example, "Because cats crawl up trees." When the answers have been written, the paper is returned to the player who wrote the original question. Then each player takes turns reading aloud both the question and answer on the paper, which is sure to bring smiles and laughter to everyone.

I Challenge It

I Challenge It requires a minimum of two players who have both reading and spelling abilities. The first player writes a letter on a sheet of paper and passes it to the next player. The second player secretly thinks of a word starting with that letter and then adds the second letter of that word on the paper. Play continues with the paper being passed along to other players, each adding a letter to create a word, until no player can add another letter to form a word. For example, if the first player writes *l*, the second player writes *i*, and players continue adding letters until the word becomes *likes*; play ends with the player adding the *s*, as there are no more letters that can be added to this word. If on their turn, a player cannot add another letter, he is out of the game. The last player remaining is the winner. Players can challenge each other if they think a player does not have a word in mind but adds a letter anyway. For instance, if a player adds a *y* to the *l* and another player does not think there is any word that start with the letters *ly*, she can challenge. If that player can spell the word correctly, such as *lying*, he wins the game.

Head, Shoulders, Knees, and Toes

Head, Shoulders, Knees, and Toes is played by a minimum of two players. Each player begins by drawing a head and neck of a person or animal on the top third of a sheet of paper. Then players fold over their paper so just the neck they've drawn is showing. Next, everyone passes the drawing to the player on their right. Without unfolding them, the next player draws a body with legs in the center third of the paper, starting at the neck lines. When finished with the body, players fold their paper so just the legs are showing: Again, players pass these papers to the player on their right. Finally, players draw feet, joining the leg lines. When finished, all drawings are returned to the player who started the original drawing.

Scrambled Letters

Scrambled Letters needs at least three players, and one is the caller. The caller assigns nine letters, including at least two vowels, for all players to use during each round of play. Each player writes down the letters on a sheet of paper and tries to think of the longest word possible using only those letters. The player creating the longest word wins the game. For example, if the caller gives the letters *b*, *r*, *t*, *p*, *m*, *n*, *g*, *a*, and *e*, and one player writes *ant*, another writes *rent*, and the last player writes *parent*, the last player wins because he used the most letters.

> Variation: For more complicated scoring, the winning player receives one point per letter or double points if all nine letters are used.

Consequences

Consequences is played by a minimum of two players, each having a piece of paper. Each player writes the same phrase to start a story on the top of the paper, such as "On a dark and stormy night," "Once upon a time," or "In a land far, far away." Then players fold their paper to hide the phrase and pass it to the next player, who continues the story according to the following steps. Words in parentheses are replaced by words or phrases chosen by each player. After each line of the story, the paper is folded again and passed to the next player.

1. (A man or boy's name)
2. met (a woman or girl's name)
3. in/at/on (where they met)
4. He said (what he said)
5. She said (what she said)
6. He (what he did)
7. She (what she did)
8. So here's what happened . . .

When the players have completed all eight steps, papers are returned to the original writer, unfolded, and the finished stories are read one at a time for everyone to enjoy.

> Variation: For players with little or no writing ability, having a partner with writing skills to write their ideas keeps them involved in the game.

Jumbled Words

Jumbled Words needs at least two players, and it is best for them to have spelling and reading skills. One player is the leader. The goal is for players to unscramble each other's list of jumbled words the fastest. Each player makes a list of ten five-letter words, scrambling the order of the letters. For example, happy can be written as payph, or start can be written as trats. On the leader's "Go" signal, players try to unscramble their page of words. The first player to finish says, "Done." At that time all players stop their work and read their unscrambled words. Players score one point for each correctly written word, even if they were not the first player to finish. If one of the scrambled words can be unscrambled to make two or more words using the same five letters and a player writes more than one, that player receives extra points. If a player cannot unscramble a word because her opponent didn't include the right letters, the opponent loses one point for the error. The player with the most points at the end of the game is the winner.

Works of Art

Works of Art is played by a minimum of three players, each with a blank sheet of paper. The goal of this game is for each player to create a work of art incorporating the suggestions of all of the players. Time allotted for drawing objects should be based on players' abilities. The first player names an person, animal, or object. All players draw this on their paper. When all players are finished drawing the first item named, it's the next player's turn to name something to add to the drawing. This continues until all players have had a turn to choose an item to be drawn.

Guess My Word

Guess My Word needs at least four players divided into equal teams. The first team secretly writes a word known by all players, such as an animal, person, or object. One player from the opposing team is chosen as the artist and is shown the word. A time limit of one minute begins, and the artist draws a picture of the word, trying to get other members of his team to guess the word correctly. The artist is not allowed to give clues by talking or by drawing letters or symbols. If the word is guessed correctly within the time limit, the team scores one point, and it is the other team's turn to draw a word. If the word is not guessed correctly within the time limit, no points are scored and play passes to the other team. After both teams have had an equal number of turns to get a predetermined number of points, the first team to reach that total is the winner. In case of a tie, a "draw-off" is needed.

Obstruction

Obstruction is played with two players. Before play begins, a set of thirty-six connected squares is drawn on a paper in a grid, six down and six across. More squares can be added to extend the play or when the game is played by players who enjoy more of a challenge. One player is O, and the other is X. Players take turns writing their letter in a square only if all the adjoining squares are empty. The first player unable to mark a square loses.

Word Gallery

Word Gallery needs at least two players with reading and spelling skills. The goal is to write words in a way that letters of the words create a visual of the word, such as the examples here. Players take turns choosing a word for other players to draw.

underline   fall ng   sun   bigger
                      i   set

Play continues until all players have had a turn to choose a word to illustrate. There are no winners or losers, just lots of creative fun.

Lines of Designs

Lines of Designs is a two-player game requiring crayons, markers, or colored pencils. Before the game begins, one player draws a free-form line design that completely covers a sheet of paper. This design should have many lines that intersect. Players choose a color as their own and take turns shading in an area on the design. No two touching areas can be the same color. The winner is the last player able to shade in an area not touching another area that is hers.

Letter Tic-Tac-Toe

Letter Tic-Tac-Toe needs a minimum of two players. A standard Tic-Tac-Toe board is drawn on a sheet of paper by making a three-by-three open grid, each spot with a letter in it. To begin the game, each player has a marker, crayon, pen, or pencil of a color that is different from the other player. The first player chooses a letter from the board and says any word that begins with that letter. Then the next player names a word that begins with the same letter. Play continues back and forth until no player can think of another word that begins with the chosen letter. The player who gives the last successful answer gets to circle the letter on the board in his color and chooses the next letter on the grid to play. As in Tic-Tac-Toe rules, the first player to circle three letters in a row in any direction wins the game.

Number Maze

Number Maze needs a minimum of two players. Two sets of numbers from one to twenty are written in a random manner on a piece of paper. Each player chooses a different color of writing utensil, which will be hers for the game. Players take turns trying to connect two of the same number using a straight line without crossing their line over another line on the page. The winner is the player with the most connected pairs of numbers.

All Ways

All Ways is played by a minimum of two players with reading and spelling skills. One player says the name of a person, animal, or object, which is then written in the center of each player's paper. Players are given a specified amount of time to build other words from the letters in the chosen word, either in a horizontal or vertical manner. All new words must be related in some way to the chosen word. For example, if the word *umbrella* was chosen, a player's answers could look like this:

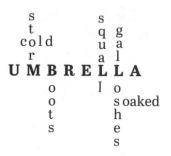

```
        s           s
        t           q    g
      cold          u    a
        r           a    l
      U M B R E L L A
        o           I    o
        o           s oaked
        t           h
        s           e
                    s
```

The player with the most words wins.

> Note: Using a longer word (such as *umbrella*, *football*, or *wintertime*) works best for this game.

Cram, Also Called Plugg

Cram, or Plugg, is a game for two players with different colors of writing utensils. Before the game begins, players need a grid of any number of dots spread across and down a sheet of paper. Players take turns connecting any two dots, either horizontally or vertically. No two dots can be connected to each other more than once. The first player unable to connect two dots loses the game.

> Variation: One player can make only vertical lines and the other can make only horizontal lines; no dots can be connected to each other more than once.

Letters and Words

Letters and Words needs a minimum of two players, each with a sheet of paper. One player is the leader and chooses a letter to start the game. During a predetermined time limit, each player writes down as many words that start with the chosen letter as they can. Players with limited spelling skills may choose to draw their answers. The winner is the player with the most correctly spelled words or drawn pictures beginning with the chosen letter when time is up.

> **Variation:** A more challenging variation is to pick a category for each letter, such as places, animals, or people. All items on the list must fit the category and the chosen letter.

The Name Game

The Name Game requires at least two players, each with a sheet of paper. One player chooses a word, and all players write it down the left side of their page, one letter under another. Then players are given a few minutes (five or less) to write as many first names as they can think of that begin with the letters in the word written down the side of their page. One point is given for each commonly used or creative name. Even the wild and wacky names score a point. The winner is the player with the most points at the end of the round.

Mythical Creatures

Mythical Creatures is played by a minimum of two players, who can be introduced to the idea of creating their own extraordinary creatures by learning about some of mythology's famous beasts.

- Pegasus: a winged horse
- Sphinx: head of a person and body of a lion
- Unicorn: a small white horse with a long, straight horn between its ears
- Dragon: a huge reptile that snorts fire and has a massive tail

Players use paper and markers to draw their own mythical creature and write descriptions or stories about it. After all players have finished their mythical creatures, it's time for Show and Tell. No losers in this game—just creativity at its best.

> **Note:** It's important that players realize not all creatures are frightening just because of their looks or size.

Snakes

Snakes needs at least two players with a writing utensil of a different color. Before the game begins, a grid of dots, of a minimum of five rows down and five rows across (twenty-five dots), is drawn on a sheet of paper. Players take turns creating their own snake by drawing a straight line in any direction, connecting a dot to any neighboring dot. Their lines cannot touch their opponent's snake or another line on their own snake. The first player unable to move to the next dot loses.

Reverse Tic-Tac-Toe

Reverse Tic-Tac-Toe is for two players and needs a standard Tic-Tac-Toe, or three-by-three open grid, drawn on a sheet of paper. One player is *X*, and the other player *O*. As in regular Tic-Tac-Toe, players take turns writing their letter in one of the squares on the grid. The first player must take the center square. The winner is the player who does not have either three of her *X*s or *O*s in a straight row.

Alpha Bits and Pieces

This game is for two players with reading and spelling skills. Each player needs a piece of paper and a writing utensil. One player is the leader, who selects a word of at least eight letters. Both players write that word across the top of their paper. Players try to make as many other words as they can in a predetermined time limit, using only the letters in the word at the top of the paper. Letters can be used in a word as many times as they appear in the chosen word. For instance, if the word *telephone* is chosen, words that players make could include *let*, *lot*, *help*, *peel*, and *hole*. The winner is the player with the most correctly spelled words on his list at the end of the time limit.

CHAPTER 11

MEALTIME GAMES

Scrambled Words

Scrambled Words is played with a minimum of three players, each with a disposable menu. One player takes words from a menu and writes them in a scrambled way, without the other players seeing the original words. When the scrambler shows her list to everyone, players try to unscramble the words and circle them on their menu. The first player to unscramble all words is the winner.

The list here includes mealtime words and can be used for this game when menus are not available. To help players be successful, words used in this game should be appropriate to players' reading skills.

hamburger	*brrumhage*
pickles	*lipscke*
french fries	*herfnc efsir*
ice tea	*eic eat*
corn	*norc*
dessert	*etsdser*
sandwich	*wadihcns*
bread	*erdab*
bacon	*cnaob*
cheese	*ehesce*

David's Dots

David's Dots is played by two players. Before the game begins, one player draws a three-by-three open grid with nine dots, three dots across and three dots down, on a piece of paper, paper napkin, or paper placemat. Dots should be about three inches apart. One player selects three sugar or sugar substitute packets in a single color. The other player chooses three packets in a different color; two different types of coins can be used if these are not available. The goal of the game is to be the first player to get three packets in a row (straight across, straight down, or diagonally). Players take turns until all packets are on dots. If a player puts three of his packets in a row, he wins. If neither player has three in a row, the first player slides one of his packets onto a dot adjacent to any of his other packets; however, he cannot pick up a packet to jump over a packet on a dot. Players take turns moving their pockets until one player has three packets in a row and wins the game.

Cup Toss

Cup Toss needs at least two players, empty plastic cups, and paper napkins. Players crinkle a small amount of paper napkin into a tight ball and take turns trying to get the paper ball into the cups. Points are given for each successful dunk in the cup. This game can be played individually, or players can be grouped into teams. The player or team with the highest score after a predetermined amount of time is the winner.

Now You See It, Now You Don't

Now You See It, Now You Don't needs a minimum of two players; three sweetener packets of the same color, such as yellow sugar substitute, white sugar, or blue sweetener; and a small coin. This is the mealtime version of the cups and balls magic trick. One player is the magician. The rules of the game are simple. The magician places the coin under one packet and shows the others which packet the coin is under. Then the magician quickly mixes around all of the packets while everyone watches. The goal is to see if anyone can follow the coin and find it under one of the packets after the shuffling is complete. The player who guesses where the coin is gets the next turn to hide it.

Straw Wrapper Worms

Straw Wrapper Worms is played by a minimum of two players. Each player needs a straw wrapped in paper. As players unwrap their straws, they scrunch up the paper wrappers, then lay them on the table. As a drop of water is put on the crinkles of each one, they wiggle and grow. For additional fun, a course can be set for the worms to follow or players can predict which direction they'll go or grow.

Letter Spies

Letter Spies needs a minimum of two players and a disposable menu. One player chooses a letter of the alphabet and asks all other players to circle the letter wherever it is found on the menu. When players think they have found all the letters, each player counts up his total. The player who has found the most letters wins the round and selects the next letter to be circled on the menu. Younger players can be shown the designated letter for them to match.

> **Variation: Numbers one through ten can be substituted for letters.**

What's Gone?

What's Gone needs at least three players. One player arranges a group of objects, such as different types of sweetener packets, eating utensils, salt or pepper shakers, or other objects, and puts them in the middle of the table. Then players are given a set period of time to memorize the items they see. When the time is up, players cover their eyes, and the first player removes one object from the table and says, "What's gone?" Then other players open their eyes and try to be the first to guess the missing item. The first player to get the correct answer is the winner and has the next turn to be the arranger of the items.

Picasso on a Placemat

Picasso on a Placemat is played by a minimum of three players. All players draw a shape on the back of a paper placemat or paper napkin and then pass the placemat or napkin to the player sitting to their right. The new player adds a line, dot, or basic shape (such as a square, circle, or triangle) to the drawing. The masterpieces continue being passed with each player adding their line, dot, or shape. When it is agreed upon by all players that the masterpieces are done, it's time to color and add details. The last step is to name and admire each work of art.

> Variation: As each new line or shape is added, the player describes what she thinks the drawing is or what it looks like.

The Rainbow Connection

The Rainbow Connection needs at least three players. One player chooses a color and tells the other players the color he has chosen. Players take turns looking around the room to find objects of that color, and they call out what they see. When all players have spotted something of the first color, the next player chooses a new color. The game continues until boredom sets in or the food arrives.

Mr. Egghead

Mr. Egghead is the classic game of Hangman with a foodie twist and is played by a minimum of two players. The object is to guess the correct word before Mr. Egghead has his eyes, ears, hands, feet, eyebrows, mouth, and nose. The first player starts by thinking of a word that is known by the other players. Then she draws a line to represent each letter of the word and an egg shape at the top of the page. Players take turns guessing one letter at a time trying to spell the word. If a correct letter is guessed, it is written in the space or spaces. If a letter is not in the word, one feature of Mr. Egghead is drawn, such as an eye or ear. The game continues until the correct word is guessed or Mr. Egghead is completed without a player guessing the correct word. Tracking the incorrect letters under the letters line helps players so they don't guess the same letter more than once.

Which Hand?

Which Hand? needs at least two players. One player puts both of his hands under the table and hides a small object, such as a sugar packet or piece of a napkin, in one hand, then makes a fist with both. Then he shows his fists and asks the other players which hand the object is in. The first player to guess correctly wins the game and gets the next turn to hide the object.

Spooning

Spooning is played by a minimum of two players, and small spoons work best. Players can breathe heavily on their spoons so they become foggy and warm (which helps the spoons stick to noses easier). Players tip their heads back and place their spoon on their nose to balance. The spoon should be placed so that it is up high on the bridge of the nose and held until it's balanced and hangs securely to the nose. It is quite a sight when all players get their spoons balanced and hanging off their noses. There are no winners or losers, just great photo opportunities.

Through the Looking Glass

Through the Looking Glass needs at least two players. Players take turns putting their faces close to a glass full of clear liquid and make funny faces at each other. Although this game doesn't last long, it does bring lots of smiles and giggles.

Money Talks

Money Talks is played by a minimum of two players and one denomination of paper money, such as one dollar or five dollar bills. If players use real money, after the game is over, all money should be given back to its owner. Each player needs a bill.

Players take turns asking others to find certain objects on the bill, such as an eye in a triangle, the head of an eagle, thirteen arrows, images of Abraham Lincoln, places where the number five is located, or twenty stars and thirteen stripes. Items can be adjusted according to the abilities of the players as well as the type of money available. Coins work for this guessing game too.

Mirror Images

Mirror Images needs a minimum of two players and works well when two players sit opposite each other across a table. Additional players should be paired together, or if there is an uneven number of players, three can play together, one player being the face-maker and the others the mirror. The first player begins the game by initiating an action or gesture such as scratching her head, winking, or rolling her tongue. The second player must imitate the action and any others that the first player does. The goal is for both players to be mirror images of each other and do the same movement at the same time. After a minute or two of play, it's the second player's turn to lead the activity.

The Great Balancing Act

The Great Balancing Act is played by a minimum of two players. Small packets of sugar, jelly, ketchup, or sauces are needed. Players take turns respectfully handling and trying to balance as many packets as they can on one finger. All players should use the same finger as each other, such as the pointer, thumb, or ring finger.

> Variations: Players try to balance a drinking straw on a finger, or players try to balance packets on more than one finger at the same time.

My Senses Say

My Senses Say needs at least two players and is similar to I Spy with My Little Eye (page 50), only using more than just the sense of sight. Mealtimes are full of smells, sounds, and tastes, so they are perfect times to play this game. As a group, players decide on a sense of sight, sound, smell, or taste before the start of the game. One player (the Spier) identifies an item using the chosen sense and gives hints to other players to help them guess the item. For instance, a player may say, "I smell a food that everyone likes to eat with hamburgers" or "I see something that is cold and sweet." Players take turns guessing the selected food; the first player to guess correctly wins the game and gets to be the spier for the next round of play.

How Much Longer?

How Much Longer? is played by a minimum of two players. This is a perfect game when everyone's hungry or when you are waiting for food to arrive. All players guess how long it will take for everyone to be served their meals. No two players can choose the same length of time. The winner is the player who guesses closest to actual time the food is served.

Stacks and Straws

Stacks and Straws needs at least two players, four drinking straws, and a variety of types of sugar and sugar substitute packets, which are distributed to players by color. Players should have an equal number of packets. Straws create a grid of open squares on the table large enough for one packet in each space. Players take turns placing one of their packets in an open space on the grid or covering another player's packet with one of theirs. This can be done by using a new packet or by moving one of their packets already on the board from one space to another. The first player to have four of his packets showing anywhere on the board wins the game.

> Variation: Drinking straws can be used to create a Tic-Tac-Toe board and packets used as space markers instead of drawing Xs or Os. The first player with three packets in a row is the winner.

Bubbles? No Trouble!

In Bubbles? No Trouble! players hold a cup upright and insert a straw deep into either water, lemonade, iced tea, or milk, then blow gently into the straw to create bubbles in their drink. Fizzy drinks should not be used for this game, or there will be bubbles on the table and undoubtedly everyone sitting close by.

Taste and Tell

Taste and Tell is played by three or more players, one of whom is the leader. After players have received their meals, a spoon is collected for each player. The leader takes all of the spoons and instructs other players to close their eyes. Then she puts a very small amount of something from her meal on a separate plate and uses that plate to put a little onto each of the spoons. The spoons are given back to each player. With their eyes still closed, players taste the food on their spoon; even a just a quick lick of the food is acceptable. Then players guess what they have just tasted. The first player to guess correctly is the winner and is the next player to be the leader.

Spoon It Out

Spoon It Out needs at least three players, each with a spoon, and a sugar or condiment packet. More capable players hold the spoon in their nondominant hand. The first player puts a sugar packet in his spoon and tries to pass it carefully into the spoon of the next player without it falling off. The goal of this game is for players to work together to pass the packet to all players without it being dropped. If it falls off of the spoons, the player who tried to pass it puts the packet back on his spoon and starts over.

> Variation: This game could be played by two players. Players can challenge each other to see how long they can pass the packet between them without dropping it.

Menu Mysteries

Menu Mysteries is played by a minimum of three players, each with the same disposable menu and a writing utensil. One player chooses a word that can be found on the menu and asks other players to circle the word on the menu as many times as it appears. For players with limited reading ability, the word can be written down and visible so they can use it to match with letters. Sometimes the mystery word is located within other words, such as when *ice* appears in *iced tea*, *rice*, or *ice cream*.

> **Variation:** A mystery number or symbol such as $, +, or *, is selected to be found on the menu.

Read My Lips

Read My Lips requires at least two players. One player is the leader and writes down a word known by all players on a sheet of paper without other players seeing it. Then the leader silently mouths the word to the other players. Players take turns guessing what word the leader is mouthing. The first player to guess correctly gets the next turn to be the leader.

Placemat Portrait Studio

Placemat Portrait Studio is played by a minimum of two players. The back of a paper placemat is perfect for drawing portraits or caricatures of others in the group. Each player chooses another player to sketch and sets to work with pencils, crayons, or any other drawing tools available. No two players should sketch the same person to ensure that everyone in the group is the subject of a portrait. When the portraits are complete, these are shared with the group.

CHAPTER 12

SEASONAL GAMES

Autumn Games

Balancing Backs

Balancing Backs is played by a minimum of five players. One player is the leader. All other players divide into two equal teams. If one team has fewer players, one player will have two turns. Before the game begins, a starting and finish line are marked and known by all players. Each player chooses a fall object such as an acorn, pinecone, small twig, small rock, leaf, or other object that will be balanced on his lower back during the race. Team players line up single file on their hands and knees behind the starting line. At the leader's "Go" signal, the first player in line balances her object on her back and crawls to the finish line. If her object falls off, she can put it back on her back and continue. When a player successfully crosses the finish line, the leader tells the next player in that player's team to start. The first team with all players crossing the finish line wins the game.

> **Variation: All players balance their fall object on their head and walk to the finish line.**

All for Fall Rescue

All for Fall Rescue calls for at least seven players. One player is the leader. All other players divide into two teams, and it's okay if a team has one more player. This game requires a large open playing area marked and divided in half. Each team takes one side of the playing area. Before the game begins, all players find fall objects and leave these at the end line of the opposing team. To recover these fall treasures, a team has to cross into the other team's side, take their objects and run back, on the leader's "Go" signal. Each player can get any object in his team's pile. Any tagged player must return the object he was carrying and is out of the game. All tagged players stand behind their team's pile of treasures, while players not tagged run with their object to their home base. After any member of the first team is tagged, the leader instructs the other team to go. Players can choose to save one of their teammates rather than bring back an object from their team pile by tagging them back in. The team to collect the most treasures before all of their teammates are tagged is the winner.

Leaf, Leaf, Nut

Leaf, Leaf, Nut is played by a minimum of four players. One player is It. Players sit in a circle while the player who is It stands outside of the circle and holds a small nut (or pinecone). The player who is It holds the nut in one hand and touches the heads of other players with his other hand saying, "Leaf, leaf, leaf." He then chooses a player to tap her head and say, "Nut," dropping the nut behind that player's back. The player stands up with the nut and tries to catch and tag the player who is It before he sits down in the open spot in the circle. If the player catches It, she keeps her spot in the circle, and It continues with another round of play. If It successfully reaches the player's space in the circle, the chased player is the new It. Play continues until all players have had the opportunity to be It for a round of play.

The Scarecrow Says

The Scarecrow Says needs at least three players and is the same as Simon Says (page 55), with one player, the scarecrow, giving the commands. Players follow his directions, but only if he begins his commands with "Scarecrow says." If the scarecrow does not begin his commands this way, players do not obey. Any player who does not follow the rules correctly is out of the game. The last player to remain in the game is the winner and becomes the new scarecrow.

Piles and Smiles Race

Piles and Smiles Race can be played by a minimum of two players outdoors in a place where leaves are scattered on the ground. One player is the leader. The other players divide into two teams; it's okay if one team has more players. Two equal-sized, large circles are drawn on the ground by the leader. When the leader says "Go," all players gather up leaves in their hands to put into their team's circle before the leader counts to twenty (or more). After the leader has finished counting, the team with the most leaves in its pile wins.

Football Call Ball

Football Call Ball needs at least five players. One player is the quarterback, while the other players are the receivers. Each receiver is given a different number. When the game is ready to begin, the receivers stand in a line in front of the quarterback. The quarterback throws a football in the air and calls out a number. The player with that number tries to catch the ball before it hits the ground. If she is successful, she becomes the new quarterback, and the previous quarterback gets that player's number. If she doesn't catch the ball, the player goes back into the line and the quarterback continues throwing the ball into the air until a player catches it.

> Variation: The quarterback calls any number ending with either a five or a zero between zero and fifty (for example, twenty-five, ten, forty). After the ball is thrown, any receiver can catch the ball and gets that number of points. The first player to reach one hundred points becomes the next quarterback.

Leaf Race

Leaf Race is played by a minimum of three players, each of whom chooses a dried leaf from the ground. Flat ones with curled edges work best. One player is the leader. A starting line and finish line are marked on the ground approximately ten to fifteen feet apart, depending on players' abilities. All players except the leader line up side by side, on their hands and knees at the starting line, with their leaves touching the starting line. At the leader's "Go," players try to blow their leaves toward the finish line without touching them. The first player to get his leaf across the finish line is declared "The Strongest Fall Wind."

> **Variations:** An obstacle course can be added for players to blow the leaves around or through. Play can be extended by having the leaves blown to the finish line and back to the starting line.

 ## Squirrels in the Tree

Squirrels in the Tree needs a minimum of eleven players. One player is the leader, and the other players divide into groups of three. This game should be played in an area large enough for everyone to move safely without bumping into each other. In each group of three, two players hold hands and lift their arms to form trees. The third player is the squirrel and starts the game standing between his two trees. The other players are the extra squirrels without a home and are positioned anywhere in the playing area that is not close enough to touch a tree. When the game begins, the leader shouts "Change" and claps her hands. All squirrels (both in the trees and extras) run to find a new tree; only one squirrel is allowed in each tree. The squirrels left out become the new extra squirrels and the leader shouts "Change" again. Squirrels and trees are rotated often to give everyone a chance to play.

> **Variation:** For a more challenging game, squirrels play the game on their hands and knees, hop, or slide between trees.

Fall Relay

Fall Relay is played by a minimum of five players. One player is the leader, and the other players divide into two equal teams. If there is an uneven number of players, one player from the smaller team has two turns. Each team has a spoon and an acorn or other size-appropriate nut in a shell placed on the ground in front of the first players on each team. When the leader says "Go," the first players on each team scoop the nut off the ground using their spoon and walk as fast as they can around a designated marker and back again. They pass the spoon and nut to the next player in line to continue the relay race. If a player drops the nut, he must stop, pick it up, and place it on the spoon before continuing on the course. The winning team is the first to have all its players complete the course.

> **Note:** If nuts are not available or a player has a nut allergy, unpopped kernels of popcorn, small pebbles, dice, or marbles can be substituted.

Winter Games

Snowman Follow the Leader

Snowman Follow the Leader needs at least three players in a large, snowy open space. One player is the snowman, and without the other players looking, makes footprints in the snow in a variety of ways such as crisscross (scissor steps), hopping on one foot or both feet, taking steps with big or very small strides, or walking in a zigzag manner. When the snowman has finished making tracks across the playing area, other players must follow in the snowman's footsteps without making new ones of their own. After all players have followed the snowman's footprints, he can select a new snowman. The game will have to move to another snowy area free of tracks or footprints for each round of play. The game continues until all players have had a turn to be the snowman.

All Dressed Up

All Dressed Up needs at least five players for a relay or three for an individual race. If played as a relay, one player is the leader, and the other players divide into two equal teams with the same type and number of clothing pieces, such as hats, gloves or mittens, boots, coats, and scarves. If there is an uneven number of players, one player on a team with fewer players has two turns. Players sit side by side with their team. The leader says "Go," and the first player in each team's line stands up and puts on all the clothing as quickly as possible and when finished says, "Ready." At that point, they remove the items they have put on, pass them to the next player in their line, and then sit down at the end of the line. The next player in line stands up and puts on all of her winter clothing. The first team that has all players finished putting on all of their clothing items wins.

If this game is played individually, the leader gives the "Go" signal, at which time all players start putting on the same type and number of outdoor clothing items. When a player is finished, she sits down. The first player to sit is the first-place winner (but the game continues with more players declared in second place and so on until all players are dressed and ready to go outside).

 ## Colorful Touches

Colorful Touches is played by a minimum of five players. All players except one, the caller, stand in a circle at least an arm's length between each other, with their shoes off. The caller stands in the middle of the circle and says either "foot" or "hand," followed by a color. For example, "Left hand, blue." Each player touches his left hand to an article of his clothing that is blue. If he is not wearing any blue clothing items, he should place his left hand on something blue another player is wearing. Because players cannot move from their place in the circle, they must stretch or bend to touch another player. If players lose their balance or cannot reach a player standing close enough to touch from where they are, they are out of the game and sit down to become spectators. The last player remaining in the circle is the winner and becomes the new caller.

Sock Skating

Sock Skating needs a minimum of two players in a carpet-free playing area. Players put socks over their shoes or remove their shoes and wear only their socks. Then players move their bodies in a skating motion (sliding their feet) without bumping into other players. Depending on the ability of players, they can try spins or hockey stops or see who can slide the farthest. The game continues until all skaters are exhausted or lose interest in the game.

> Note: To ensure safety, it is best to have a skating coach or skating supervisor who ensures players move cautiously and cooperatively. A penalty box, similar to those found in hockey games, may be necessary to remove out-of-control skaters for a short time. The area used for playing this game must be open, free of furniture, and be a hard surface without splinters or irregularities.

Freeze Frame

Freeze Frame needs at least five players, each with a small book or beanbag. One player is the leader. On the leader's "Go" signal, players try to balance their book or beanbag on their head as they move around an open playing area, without bumping into other players. If the object on a player's head falls off, that player is frozen. Another player can help thaw this player by picking up the object and putting it back on the player's head without losing her own object. When the leader announces the game is over, the player who has unfrozen the most other players is the winner, is thanked by all other players, and is the leader for the next round of play.

> Variation: To make the game more challenging, the leader can ask players to hop or skip.

Columns

Columns calls for a minimum of two players outdoors in the snow. All players work together to make a row of snow mounds about six inches high and three inches around (about the size of an adult's hand) and leave a space about the length of an adult's foot between each mound. When these are complete, players take five steps back from this snow row and take turns tossing any sized snowball they have made at the mounds. Each time a player hits a mound with a snowball, she gets a point. The game continues until all mounds have been knocked over. The player with the most points after all of the mounds are knocked over is the winner.

 ## Snowball Toss

Snowball Toss is played by at least two players in a snowy area. One player draws a circle in the snow with a small twig or other object. The size of the circle can vary depending on the ability of the players. To simplify the game, the circle should be about three feet in diameter, while a smaller circle is more challenging. Then players stand the same distance away from the circle. Players take turns making a snowball and tossing it so it lands inside the circle. Players score a point for a snowball tossed inside the circle. The first player to reach a predetermined number of points wins the game.

 ## Snow Angels

Snow Angels is played by a minimum of two players in snow free of tracks or footprints, with everyone dressed from head to toe in waterproof clothing. Players make snow angels by lying on their backs in the snow. Then they wave their arms above their heads and back down to their waists to make wings and move their legs out and back to create the angel's skirt. Snow angels are best created when a player gets help standing up so as not to put any additional footprints in the snow.

 ## Bigfoot Snow Boot

Bigfoot Snow Boot needs at least three players in a snowy area without any footprints or tracks in it. Before the game begins, the playing area and home base are defined and known to all players. One player is bigfoot. Other players stay at the designated home base, turn their back to bigfoot and the playing area, and slowly count to fifty. Bigfoot moves away from the other players, leaving footprints in many directions by walking backward, hopping on one foot, and other motions. When players are done counting, they set out to find bigfoot by following his tracks. If he can get back to the home base without being seen, he is saved. If bigfoot is seen or caught, the player who finds him becomes the next bigfoot. The game will have to move to another snowy area free of tracks or footprints for each round of play.

The Fox and the Geese

The Fox and the Geese is played by a minimum of four players outdoors in a snowy place. One player is the leader. Before the game begins, the leader draws a ten-to-twenty-foot circle in the middle of an open playing area with a twig or other object. The circle is divided into at least four but not more than eight pieces in a sliced-pie form. One player is the fox, and all other players are the geese. All players, both the fox and the geese, need to stay on the lines drawn in the snow. If the leader sees players not staying on the lines, they are disqualified from the game. The leader signals "Go," and the fox chases the geese, trying to tag them. The fox and the geese can move in any direction on the lines or hop across from one line to another. They are safe from the fox if they stand in the center of the circle where all lines intersect, but only one goose can be in the center at any time. If a second goose enters the center, the first one must leave and hope to escape the fox. If a goose is caught, the roles are reversed and the goose becomes the fox, and the fox becomes a goose.

Jack Frost and the Sun

Jack Frost and the Sun is played by a minimum of five players outdoors in the snow. One player is Jack Frost, and another player is the sun. At Jack Frost's "Go," signal, all players pretend to take a winter wonderland trip and move around an open playing area in one of the following ways: pretend skiing (sliding their feet), twirling, skipping, or walking normally. Jack Frost moves among them, trying to catch and tag the other players. If players are painted (tagged) with Jack's magic paintbrush (which can be a paintbrush, small twig, or even Jack's pointer finger), they freeze in their position. As players are frozen, the sun rushes to thaw them out with a gentle touch so they may continue on their travels. Play continues as long as there is interest from the players. To keep all players interested, it's best to switch out the role of Jack Frost often.

Spring Games

The Frog Says

The Frog Says needs at least three players and is the same as Simon Says (page 55), with the frog giving the commands. Players must follow his directions but only if he begins his commands with "Frog says." If the frog does not begin his commands this way, players do not obey. Any player who does not follow the rules correctly is out of the game. The last player to remain in the game is the winner and becomes the new frog.

Rain

Rain is played by a minimum of four players sitting in a circle. One player is the leader, who starts the game by rubbing his hands together. The player to his right does the same, then the player to her right, and so on until all players are doing the action. When all players are rubbing their hands, the leader starts a new action, finger snapping, then hand clapping, slapping thighs, and then foot stomping. As the leader starts each new action, players copy the action one at a time moving around the circle counterclockwise. Creating all of these sounds in sequential order creates a rainstorm. To end the storm, the actions are done in reverse order, starting with foot stomping and ending with players rubbing their hands. At the end, starting with the leader, players one by one stop rubbing their hands and sit and wait for the rainstorm to be over. Then the leader gestures a rainbow has come out by joining his hands over his head—a smile adds to the rainbow effect too.

Rainy Day Obstacle Course

Rainy Day Obstacle Course can be played by any number of players and a large playing area free of tripping or safety hazards. What is included in the obstacle course depends on the ability of the players. Options include the following:

- Chairs to make a tunnel to crawl through
- A rolled-up towel or blanket to balance on
- A table to crawl under
- Empty water bottles set in a zigzag pattern to weave between while crawling on hands and knees
- A broom or lightweight plastic pole over chairs to slide beneath
- A blanket over chairs to make a tent to rest for a while
- Washcloths or other small pieces of cloth to create lilypads to leap from place to place

Players take turns going through one at a time at their own speed and according to their own abilities. Every player is a winner after finishing. The course can be changed or redesigned to keep players interested and challenged.

> Note: Additional rainy day games are located in the appendix.

Seeds and Sprouts

Seeds and Sprouts is played by a minimum of five players. One player is the sun. All players except the sun curl up into a ball on the floor as tightly as they can, pretending to be a small seed. The sun moves from seed to seed, touching each player gently on his back. After a player is touched, he lets his body slowly open up and reach toward the sky. When all seeds have sprouted, the sun sets (curls into a ball on the floor) and the seeds do likewise. The cycle is repeated with the sun rising and moving faster to touch each seed, which also grow more quickly. The sprouting cycle is repeated until the seeds jump into the air when the sun touches them. The game is over, and all sprouts hug together as a springtime flower bouquet.

The Wind Blows and Knows

The Wind Blows and Knows needs at least ten players. One player is the wind. All players except the wind sit in a circle, arm's length apart, and the wind stands in the center of the circle. The game begins when the wind twirls in a circle and waves his arms saying, "The March wind blows and knows . . ." At this point, the wind describes something that is true of some players, such as "The March wind blows and knows everyone with brown eyes." All players with brown eyes (or whatever the wind mentioned), stand up and try to change places with another player in the circle who has stood up. At the same time, the wind rushes to one of the open spots and tries to sit there. One player will be left standing. She becomes the wind, and the game continues as long as players are interested or have energy to be blown around by the March wind.

Toot Flute

Toot Flute is for any number of players. Tender grass and two thumbs are all that are needed to make a grass flute. Players squeeze a long blade of grass between both thumbs, hold tightly, and blow in the opening between the knuckles of the thumbs. Playing the Toot Flute takes some practice, but after players are successful, it is a musical reminder of spring.

Trees and Knees

Trees and Knees needs a minimum of six players. All players except two (who make the bridge) sit in pairs, side by side on the ground with their hands on top of their heads, fingers pointing upward; these players are growing trees. The two players who are the bridge hold each other's hands over their heads and walk together over the players who are trees, without touching any part of them. If they are successful, they call out, "Trees, on your knees if you please." At that point, all trees move from a sitting position to their knees with hands still on their heads, hands pointing upward and fingers outstretched. Again, the bridge walks over the line of trees without touching any part of them. If they are successful this time, they call out, "Trees, off your knees if you please." The players who are trees shift from their knees to a squatting position, and the bridge tries to move over them. After each successful pass through the trees, the trees continue to grow. After squatting, the trees move to a standing position and then on to their tiptoes. The bridge players continue to go through the trees trying to figure out how they can stretch taller to pass while still holding their hands together over their heads. If the bridge players touch any of the trees, they become trees, and the tree pair touched becomes the new bridge for the next round of play.

Baby Chicks

Baby Chicks is played by a minimum of five players. One player is the mother hen. At the start of the game, the mother hen either leaves the playing area or covers her eyes. When she is out of sight, two players are silently chosen by the other players to be baby chicks. Then all players sit down, put their head down, and cover their mouth with their hands. At this point, the baby chicks begin to quietly peep, with their hands still covering their mouth. The mother hen returns or opens her eyes and calls out, "Cluck, cluck" as she starts to look for her chicks. Players chosen to be chicks quietly reply, "Cheep, cheep" while keeping their mouths covered. If mother hen thinks she finds a chick, she taps him on the shoulder. If she's right, the chick picks up his head; if a player tapped is not a chick, he keeps his head down. Mother hen continues listening and looking for chicks as long as she hears one peeping. When both chicks have been found, it's time to start another round of play with a new mother hen and new baby chicks.

The Wind and the Flowers

The Wind and the Flowers needs at least five players. One player is the leader, and the other players divide into two teams, the flowers and the wind. Before the game begins, the flowers secretly agree on the name of a flower for their team name, such as rose, daisy, or petunia. In the playing area, two home base lines are marked on opposite sides. At the beginning of the game, each team stands facing the other, behind the home base lines. When the leader says "Go," the flowers move around the playing area by hopping, skipping, or dancing, closer and closer to where the wind is waiting behind the team home base line. The wind players call out names of flowers. When the flower team's secret name is called out, the flowers run back to their home base line, trying not to get tagged by wind players who chase them. Tagged players join the wind team, and a new name is chosen by the remaining flowers. When all the flowers are caught or the wind gives up (because they cannot guess the flowers' team name), the two original teams change places, with the wind becoming the flowers and the flowers becoming the wind.

I Spy Spring

I Spy Spring is played by a minimum of two players. One player is the leader. This game is similar to I Spy with My Little Eye (page 50), except everything that can be spied is a sign of spring. The leader secretly chooses a spring item that all players can see, says "I see something that's a sign of spring," and then gives a hint of what he sees. Players take turns trying to guess the correct answer. The first player to guess correctly wins and becomes the leader for the next round of play.

> **Variation:** The game can be changed to include sounds of spring or even smells of spring.

Spring Critters

Spring Critters needs a minimum of four players. One player is the leader. Players position themselves in the playing area far enough apart as not to touch each other. The leader calls out one of the animal movements listed, and all players try to move their bodies like that animal without bumping into another player.

- Worms wiggle: Players lie on their stomachs, hold arms at their sides and wiggle their bodies to move forward without using hands or elbows.
- Grasshoppers leap: Players squat down with their fingers touching the floor, jump up and forward, return to their squatting position, and continue across the playing area.

- Caterpillars creep: Players lie on their stomachs with hands at their shoulder level, lift their upper bodies by straightening their arms, bring their knees forward, then stretch their bodies out flat on their stomachs, and repeat.

- Butterflies flutter: Players move their arms up and down in a flying motion while walking, skipping, or running around the playing area.

- Bumblebees buzz: While walking or running in a flying motion all around the playing area, players hold their arms straight out at their sides and spin their arms in small circles while making a buzzing sound.

- Ducks waddle: Players squat down and grab their ankles with their hands while waddling along, one foot after the next.

> Note: The leader may need to monitor the players during the game, reminding them to move safely so no animal gets hurt.

 ## Songbirds

Songbirds is played by a minimum of five players. One player is the bird. All other players stand in a circle holding their hands above their head. The bird chooses a color and tells the other players that is the color of her feathers. Players sing or say the following verse (using the chosen feather color) as the bird skips and weaves between the players standing in the circle:

(Blue) bird, (blue) bird, through my window,

(Blue) bird, (blue) bird, through my window,

(Blue) bird, (blue) bird, through my window,

To bring me a pretty flower.

When the verse stops, the bird stands in front of the player nearest her and says, "What kind of flower do you want?" and that player answers, "I want a (kind of flower, such as a rose, marigold, or dandelion). At that point, the players say, "(Player's name) wants a (named flower)." Then that player becomes the bird and the game starts again.

Variation: For players unfamiliar with the names of flowers, a color can be substituted.

 ## Springtime Rhymes

Springtime Rhymes needs at least three players. One player is the leader. The leader initiates play by saying something bees love. The word or phrase has to rhyme with *bees*, such as "Bees love trees," at which time all other players try to make themselves look like a tree. Following this, players take turns calling out more things bees like that rhyme. For instance, a player can say, "Bees love knees," and all players touch their knees, or "Bees say please" or "Bees can sneeze." Players creatively and independently think of an action or verbalize whatever has been mentioned that bees love. Play continues until no one can think of more rhymes for bees. The game can be altered to include other things seen in the spring such as "Plants love . . ." "Bugs like . . ." or "Ducks can . . ." This is not a competitive game, just lots of creative fun.

Summer Games

 ## Octopus Tag

Octopus Tag is played by a minimum of five players. The playing area is called the ocean, and all players except one are fish. The other player is the octopus and tries to tag all the fish. At the start of the game, all fish line up side by side on one side of the ocean, while the octopus is in the center of the playing area. When the octopus calls out, "Come, fishies, come!" the fish run to the other side of the ocean, trying not to be tagged by the octopus. If some fish get to the other side without getting tagged, the game resumes with the octopus calling out to them again. If tagged, fish become seaweed and stay where they were tagged, waving their arms around to assist the octopus in tagging other fish within their reach. The last fish to be tagged becomes the next octopus.

> **Variation:** Fish can only walk in a swimming motion, while the octopus must walk while moving his arms up and down one at a time.

A Wet Limbo Stick

A Wet Limbo Stick needs at least three players and is best on a hot day when all players are in their bathing suits. All that is needed is a water hose with a nozzle that makes a steady, straight stream of water. This stream of water is the limbo stick. One player holds the hose (limbo stick) while the other players take turns trying to get under the stream of water without getting wet, walking forward with their knees bent and bending backward. When a player gets wet, he becomes a spectator or helps lower the limbo stick until there are no players who are not soaking wet. The last player to get wet has a turn to hold the hose, and the game continues after all players have had time to dry off.

> **Note:** Precautions must be made to ensure the ground is not slippery and players can get safely under the water stream without falling. Placing rubber matting or a large towel on the ground beneath the water stream can help with this.

Beach Towel Toss

Beach Towel Toss is played by a minimum of four players, in pairs. If there is an extra player, players can rotate being the ball keeper who retrieves fly away balls. Each player holds the ends of a beach towel stretched flat between them, and each pair lines up side by side with their stretched towels. Players toss and catch a lightweight ball such as a tennis ball, beach ball, or sponge ball from towel to towel. There are no losers or winners in this game; players count the number of times they can toss and catch the ball without it hitting the ground.

Variation: To make the game more challenging, the pairs move farther and farther apart from each other.

Waddle like a Duck

Waddle like a Duck needs an odd number of players (at least five). One player is the leader, and the other players divide into two equal teams. Each team stands in a single-file line at one end of the defined playing area, in preparation for a relay race. The first two players on each team put a beach ball between their legs, and at the leader's "Go" signal, move across the playing area to see if they can reach the other side and back without dropping the ball. Players may find it easier to carry the ball between their elbows instead of between their legs. If the ball is dropped, the pair has to pick it up and start over again at the starting line. The winners are the first team to have all players successfully waddle like a duck with their ball across the finish line.

Variation: If a beach ball is available for each player, all players can play the game at one time. The first player back to the starting line is the winner.

Wet, Wet, Wettest

Wet, Wet, Wettest is played by a minimum of five players in an outdoor area where players can sit comfortably on the ground in their bathing suits. Players sit in a circle, while one player who is It stands outside of the circle and holds a small container of water, a wet spongy ball, or a wet washcloth. The player who is It walks around the outside of the circle, dripping a small amount of water on players' heads. As she puts water on each player's head, she says, "Wet," "Wet," "Wet," but when she pours all the water on a player's head, she says "Wettest." The soaked player stands up and runs, trying to catch the player who is It before she sits down in the open spot in the circle. If the player catches It, he keeps his spot in the circle, and It continues with another round of wet play. If It successfully reaches the player's space in the circle, the wettest player is the new It. The new It gets more water, and play continues until everyone is so wet they can't continue.

> Note: Take care to ensure the ground is not slippery and players can get around safely without falling. Grassy or sandy areas are ideal for playing this game.

Backyard Scavenger Hunt

Backyard Scavenger Hunt needs at least two players. One player is the leader and writes a printed or pictorial list of objects that can be found outside. This is given to each player or team, along with a container for the objects collected. Then the leader gives the "Go" signal, and the hunt is on. The winner is the player or team finding all items first. Playing this game is a way to focus players on natural items often overlooked in the environment.

Surf's Up!

Surf's Up! is played by a minimum of five players. In this game, all players lie face down, side by side, spaced about a body's width apart to form a long human wave. One player, the surfer, kneels at one end of the line of players and lays his body across the wave, facedown with his arms outstretched. At this point, the wave begins to move, with two players at one end of the line rolling in the same direction. The surfer lying on top of these two players rides the wave. As the surfer's body moves to new players, they start to roll too, and the surfer continues to slide across them. When the surfer finally reaches the beach at the end of the wave, he lies down and becomes part of the wave, and the player at the front of the wave gets to try her surfing skills.

Garden Veggies

Garden Veggies needs at least seven players. One player is the farmer, and all other players are a vegetable that grows under the ground, such as a carrot, a potato, an onion, or a turnip. No more than three players have any one name, such as three carrots or three potatoes. All players of the same veggie sit in a line with their arms wrapped tightly around the waist of the player in front of them. The farmer attempts to pull out these stubborn veggies from her garden by grabbing the hands of the first player in the row and trying to pull him up to a standing position and separating him from the others. The farmer has only three attempts to pull up a veggie. If she's successful, that player stands behind the farmer with his hands wrapped tightly around the farmer's waist and helps her try to pull more veggies out of the garden. If the farmer is unsuccessful, she moves on to another type of veggie. The game continues until all veggies have been pulled out of the garden or the farmer is so exhausted she can't pull out any more (at which time a new farmer is chosen).

> Note: When this game is played with fewer players, the farmer may have only one type of veggie, and all players sit together, single file. To avoid injury, the farmer should be monitored carefully to ensure he is not pulling too hard on the arms of the other players.

 ## Silly Sand Pictures

Silly Sand Pictures is played by a minimum of two players at the beach or in a large area of wet sand. Players decide who will have the first turn to draw in the sand. That player draws only one line in the sand but tells other players, "This is going to be . . ." such as a person, animal, or object. The next player continues the drawing and the sentence started by the first player by adding just one more line and what he's added, such as, "This is going to be a (man), and this is his (head)." Each player adds to the drawing trying to make it the silliest drawing possible. When all players have had a turn and the drawing has been enjoyed, it's time to wipe it away and start again.

Holes

Holes needs a minimum of two players and requires a small area of wet sand and a small stick about the diameter of a drinking straw. Players work together to pack sand into a large mound and take turns piercing the mound with the stick. The goal of the game is to pierce through the sand mound with the stick without it collapsing. To be counted in the game, the stick must go through the mound from one side to the other. Each time a player adds a hole, the mound becomes weaker until it finally collapses. The player whose hole collapsed the mound must rebuild it for the next game.

Sit and Splash

Sit and Splash needs at least three players, all in bathing suits and with a small unbreakable cup (paper or plastic), and one large container of water. One player is the leader and stands to one side of the other players, who sit together in a line with their legs in front of the player in front of them. At the leader's "Go" signal, the first player stands up to fill her cup with water from the container, then returns to her team, sits down and holds the cup over her head. The player behind her holds his cup on his head and waits while the first player tilts her head back and, without turning around, tries to pour the water from her cup into the cup of the player behind her. That player tries to catch the water without spilling it and then follows the same procedure to the player in back of him. After a player has passed the water back, she goes to the back of the line and waits for another turn. The game is over when there's no more water in the cup, but everyone's cooled down and ready to play again.

Smiles and Similes

Smiles and Similies is played by a minimum of three players in a large playing area. One player is the leader. This game needs plenty of time for players to create and act out various similes. The leader asks the other players to perform various actions, such as hopping like a bunny, wiggling like a worm, flying like an eagle, popping like popcorn, and so on. Players take turns showing everyone their actions. The role of leader is passed from player to player.

Variation: The leader can encourage players to think of how to complete a simile by starting ones such as "Crawl like a _____," "Sizzle like the ____," "Swim like a _____."

Amazing Athletes

Amazing Athletes needs at least two players. Players think of their own variation of an outdoor sporting event (such as a track meet or the Olympics) or a crazy sport to play, such as broom and jar lid hockey, pot lid tennis, or dog toy running relay, and create rules for each sporting event. Creating both team and individual games adds variety to the event. Prizes are awarded to all participants.

Water, Water, Everywhere

Water, Water, Everywhere is played by a minimum of five players. One player is the leader. This is a game best played on a hot day when everyone has bathing suits on. The other players are divided into two teams with two large containers of water in front of each team at the starting line. If there is an uneven number of players, one player on a team with fewer players has two turns. Small empty cups, one for each player on a team, are lined up either on a table or the ground a short distance from the container of water. At the leader's "Go" signal, the first players on each team scoop up water from the container in their hands and carry it to an empty cup, trying to fill that cup. Players may take more than one turn to fill their cup. Only when a cup is full can players return to their team with their cup of water. They then go to the back of the line and the next player takes a turn. The team with all players having their cups full of water first is the winner.

CHAPTER 13

TAG GAMES

It is essential all games of tag are played in hazard-free areas large enough for players to move freely. Close supervision keeps players safe and helps to enforce the rules of the game.

Simple Tag

Simple Tag is played by a minimum of three players. In most games of Simple Tag, players are free to run anywhere they wish within a designated playing area. One player (or more if desired) is It, chases the other players, and tries to tag them. When she succeeds in tagging a player, the tagged player becomes the new It and the game continues without interruption.

Chain Tag

Chain Tag needs at least three players and is similar to Simple Tag. Here, players who are tagged link elbows with It and help tag other players but can't release elbows from any other player at any time. The chain grows until all players are caught. The last player remaining not a part of the chain is the winner.

Pair Tag

Pair Tag has a minimum of three players and has rules similar to Simple Tag. The player chosen to be It stands alone, while the other players create pairs by linking arms. It tries to join a pair by linking his arms with one of the pair. If successful, the player who did not link arms with It becomes the new It.

Safety Zone

 Safety Zone needs three players and is similar to Simple Tag. Players cannot be tagged if they are touching a tree or in another designated safe zone. But a player can stay in the safe zone only until another player enters it. Then the first player has to leave the safe zone and hope not to get tagged in the process.

Shadow Tag

Shadow Tag is played by a minimum of three players with rules similar to Simple Tag in a sunny area where players can see their shadows. After It has been chosen, she tries to tag another player's shadow by stepping on it or touching it with her hand. The player whose shadow is tagged becomes It.

Reverse Tag

Reverse Tag needs at least three players and is similar to Simple Tag. After It has been chosen, all other players close their eyes and count to twenty while It runs away. Then all players try to catch It. When a player touches It, he becomes It, and other players try to tag him after they have counted to twenty, which gives him a chance to run away.

Fainting Goat Tag

Fainting Goat Tag is played by a minimum of three players with rules similar to Simple Tag. One player is It, and the other players are goats. Goats can fall to the ground for up to ten seconds to avoid being tagged but can't fall down unless It is ten feet away or closer.

Lion's Tail Tag

Lion's Tail Tag needs at least three players and is similar to Simple Tag. One player is the leader and stands to one side of the players. All other players stand in line and hold hands. The first player in the line is the lion's head, and the last is the lion's tail. On the leader's "Go" signal, the player who's the head tries to tag the tail, while the tail moves to not get caught. When the head succeeds in catching the tail, the head becomes the tail and the next player at the front of the line becomes the new lion's head. All players must remain connected throughout the game.

Number Tag

Number Tag calls for a minimum of five players. One player is It and stands in the middle of a circle formed by the other players. Before the game begins, It gives each player a number. Then It calls out two numbers, and players with those numbers try to exchange places in the circle without being tagged. If one is tagged, that player becomes the new It and the game continues.

Stoop Tag

Stoop Tag needs at least five players. One player is It and stands in the middle of a circle formed by the other players. All players except It skip around the circle singing a short song or chant. When the song ends, players stoop down quickly to keep from being tagged. If a player is not quick enough and is tagged, that player becomes the new It, and the game continues.

Arch Tag

Arch Tag requires a minimum of ten players. All players except two stand in a line while those two form an arch by holding each other's hands over their heads. One player, the caller, stands to the side of the players in line with her back turned to them. When the caller's back is turned, the players in the line rotate walking through the arch until the caller says "Stop." When "Stop" is called, the players forming the arch drop their arms and trap a player. The trapped player stands to one side in the arch, and again, the caller turns her back to the players who then move through the arch until the caller says "Stop." At this point, the two players forming the arch again lower their arms to trap the player walking through it. When two players are trapped in the arch, they are able to leave the arch and work together to form a second arch. When there are two arches, players walk under each arch until the caller says

"Stop." As additional players are trapped, more arches are built. The last player not caught in an arch is the winner.

Ball Tag

Ball Tag is played by a minimum of three players with the same rules as Simple Tag, but the player who's It runs with a ball and must throw it at a player and hit him below the waist to tag him. If a player is hit, then he becomes It.

> Note: This game should be played only under strict adult supervision, with a sponge ball, and with the rules of hitting a player below the waist strictly enforced.

Its on the Loose

Its on the Loose needs at least five players. One player is It. When It tags another player, that player also becomes It. All players who are It must keep one arm raised over their heads to be identified as they try to tag other players. The last player caught is the winner.

Color Tag

Color Tag is played by a minimum of four players. One player is the caller. The other players are scattered around the playing area while the caller stands in the middle. The caller calls a color, and any player wearing that color tries to tag players who are not wearing that color. If players are tagged, they must walk in a crab walk (hands and feet on the floor while walking) until a new color is called. Then they are free to run and play with the other players. The game continues until exhaustion or boredom sets in.

Circle Tag

Circle Tag needs a minimum of ten players. All players but two, It and the runner, stand in a double circle (a circle inside of another circle), one player in the inner circle and another player directly behind her in the outer circle. It starts the game by chasing the runner. It tries to tag the runner before she can step in front of any player standing in the inner circle. When the runner stands in front of any player in the inner circle, the player directly behind her becomes the new runner and tries to keep from being tagged by It. If the runner is tagged, the roles are reversed, and the runner becomes It. Players stand in place throughout the game unless the runner moves in front of them while standing in the inner circle.

Freeze Tag

Freeze Tag is played by a minimum of four players, who scatter in a large playing area. One player is It. When players are tagged by It, they freeze. A frozen player may become unfrozen only by another player crawling through her legs. The object is for players to try to unfreeze other players as fast as they are frozen. If a player is frozen three times, he also becomes an It. The game ends when all players have been frozen three times.

Hug

Hug needs at least four players and is a simple game of Tag with one player being It. A player is safe from being tagged if she is hugging another player. The hugging continues only until It moves away to catch another player. Then the hugs are released and the game continues. Play continues until everyone is all hugged out.

Imitation Tag

Imitation tag is played with the same rules as Simple Tag, also needing at least three players, but It can choose the way everyone moves. For example, It may change from running to hopping or from skipping to crawling at any time during the game, and all players must imitate his style. When It succeeds in tagging a player, the tagged player becomes the new It, and the game continues without interruption.

Jump the Shot

Jump the Shot requires at least three players and a long jump rope. (A knot at the end of the rope helps it swing more easily.) One player is It. All other players form a circle in the middle of the playing area. It stands in the middle of the circle with the jump rope. It swings the rope in a circle on the ground/floor. As the rope passes them, players must jump over the rope to stay in the game. When touched by the rope, that player is tagged and drops out of the circle until the next round of play. To keep the game interesting, It may vary the speed of her swings. The game ends when all players have been tagged. The last player tagged is It for the next round of play.

Line Tag

Line Tag is played by a minimum of three players on a gym floor or similar area on which lines are marked. Line tag is played with Simple Tag rules; however, the player who is It and the players being chased can run only on the lines marked on the floor. If either the player being chased or It go off a line, the roles are reversed.

Snake Tag

Snake Tag calls for at least eight players in a sunny area where players can see their shadows. Four players link their arms together to make a chain, or the snake. One player is the starter, and on his "Go" signal, the snake runs around the playing area trying to catch as many other players as it can by forming a circle around them. As soon as a player is circled by the snake, she links arms with the players who are the snake and helps capture the remaining players.

Rhythm Tag

Rhythm Tag is played by a minimum of five players and requires music, which can either be recorded or sung by a player, the maestro. To begin play, the maestro starts or sings the music, and all other players walk around the playing area until the music stops; then they stop moving. After all players have stopped in place, everyone is It! Without taking a step, players try to tag someone else. Two players cannot tag each other, so the first tag counts. All tagged players must choose a movement different from other players who are not tagged when the music starts again. They can choose to hop, skip, jump, or crawl while all other players must walk. Each time the music stops, all players stop moving and the tagged players try to tag those not tagged. Tagged players can move any way they want when the music is playing, except to walk or run. The winner is the last walker remaining untagged.

Body Tag

Body Tag needs at least five players. The game is played with Simple Tag rules, except when It tags another player, the tagged player becomes the new It and chases other players with his hand placed on the spot of his body where he was tagged. For instance, if It touches a player on his shoulder, that player becomes It and chases other players while holding one hand on his shoulder. The pace of the game can slow down considerably when a player is tagged on the foot or part of his leg. The game ends when all players are too exhausted to continue or everyone has had a turn to be It.

CHAPTER 14

GAMES WITH SIMPLE RULES

This chapter includes games with simple rules most appropriate for children under the age of three, players with limited vocabulary, or ones with emerging language skills.

 ### Red Light, Green Light

Red Light, Green Light is played by a minimum of four players. One player is the leader and stands at one end of the playing area while all other players stand in a side-by-side line at the other end. The leader turns his back to the others and calls out "Green light!" Then players run as fast as they can toward the leader. At any point, the leader can turn and face the running players and yell out "Red light." During a red light, all players freeze in place. If a player does not stop running and the leader sees her, she returns to the starting line. The first player to reach the leader wins and becomes the leader for the next round.

Variations: This game can be played with two teams. When players are frozen in place, if a player does not stop running and the leader sees him, the entire team returns to the starting line.

Hide It Find It

Hide It Find It needs at least four players and an object about two inches big. The object is placed on the ground close by but not within reach of the player chosen to be the leader. The leader stands with her back to the other players at one end of the playing area. On the leader's "Go" signal, the other players run as a group toward the leader, trying to steal this object. When they reach the object, they all take it to the their end of the playing area and hope to hide it well enough so the leader cannot see it. When the players think it's hidden, they call out, "Find It." Then the leader turns toward the other players and has several guesses to find out who stole the object and where it is without moving from her place. If she guesses correctly, the game starts over. If she does not guess correctly, another player becomes the leader and new round of play begins.

Where Is Thumbkin?

Where Is Thumbkin? is played by a minimum of three players. At the beginning of this game, all players have both hands behind their back. As the song is sung, players show the appropriate finger on one hand. As the line is repeated, the same finger on the other hand is shown. During the next two lines, the two fingers wiggle as if talking to each other. At the last line, the fingers move behind the players' backs, one finger at a time. The song is repeated for all fingers starting with thumbkin (thumb), pointer (index finger), middle, ringer (ring finger), and pinky (little finger).

Where is (thumbkin)?

Where is (thumbkin)?

Here I am, here I am.

How are you today, sir (or ma'am)?

Variations: For a simpler game, one player can lead other players and show them the actions and fingers to use. In another version, if playing in a group, players close their eyes while another player hides in the area. Then players sing, "Where is (Connor)?" and try to guess where the player is hiding. If the player is not found after all players have had a turn to guess, the hidden player pops up saying, "Peekaboo! Here I am!"

Very well, I thank you.

Run away, run away.

Peekaboo

Peekaboo is for two players who sit face to face, one player covering her eyes with her hands. The second player says, "Where's (Sophia)? Where's (Sophia)?" at which time, the first player says, "Peekaboo! Here I am!" opens her hands, and makes a silly face. Then the players switch roles and the play continues.

> Variations: After the first player opens her hands, the second player tries to copy the first player's facial expression. In another version, while one player's eyes are closed, the opponent changes position, such as putting an arm in the air, folding his hands in front of him, or other action. When the player says, "Peekaboo! Here I am!" the first player tries to match his pose.

The Muffin Man

The Muffin Man needs at least four players. One player is It. All players other than It stand in a circle. It stands in the middle of the circle and keeps his eyes closed. As the game starts, all players in the circle move, walking together to the left (or right) and chant or sing:

Oh, have you seen the muffin man.

The muffin man, the muffin man.

Oh, have you seen the muffin man

Who lives on Drury Lane?

At the end of the song, It moves from the middle of the circle, with his eyes still closed, until he bumps into a player in the circle. Then he opens his eyes and says, "Yes, I've seen the muffin man. It's (Alex)." The player who is named becomes the new It and the game continues.

Variations: It keeps her eyes closed after she has bumped into a player and tries to guess the player touched. Other players can give hints until the correct guess is made. In another version, It remains in the center of the circle and after the players finish the song, she says or sings her own address, "I am the muffin man who lives on (Terrywood Avenue)." Players can also substitute other people or places to visit such as "Have you seen (Grandpa Jones)? . . . Who lives in (Orlando, Florida)?" "Have you seen (the President)? . . . Who lives in (Washington, DC)?"

The Hokey Pokey

The Hokey Pokey is played by a minimum of two players. All players stand in a circle and sing or say the following:

You put your (right foot) in.

You put your (right foot) out.

You put your (right foot) in and shake it all about.

You do the Hokey Pokey and you turn yourself around. (Players twirl slowly with hands in the air.)

That's what it's all about! (Players slap thighs three times, then clap hands twice, followed by raising both hands in the air.)

As each line is sung, the appropriate actions are done by all of the players in the circle. Then the song is repeated and actions change to other body parts such as arm, leg, elbow, hip, knee, hand, and finally whole self.

Variations: One player is put in the center of the circle and sung to by all other players, such as "We put Mia in . . ." and she shakes it all about." The other players join in the action as the last two lines are sung. To involve more players at one time, body features, types of shoes, and color of clothing worn can be substituted. For example, "We put (green shirts) in" or "We put (black shoes) in."

Poor Kitty

Poor Kitty needs at least four players, all but one sitting in a circle. One player is the poor kitty. He moves around the inside of the circle on his hands and knees, stopping at other players while he purrs and meows. When the kitty stops at a player, she pats the kitty on the head and says, "Poor, poor kitty." If the player petting the kitty laughs or smiles while the kitty is in front of her, she becomes the kitty. If not, the kitty continues moving around the circle, stopping at other players until someone laughs and becomes the next kitty.

Ring around the Rosie

Ring around the Rosie is played by a minimum of three players. Players hold hands and form a circle. Then they walk in the same direction as they sing the following verse:

Ring around the rosie,

A pocket full of posies.

Ashes, ashes,

We all fall down.

On the word *down*, players squat down on the ground.

> **Variation:** Players create their own action to be completed as the last line of the verse is sung, such as "We all jump up" or "We all turn around."

What Time Is It, Mr. (or Mrs.) Wolf?

What Time Is It, Mr. (or Mrs.) Wolf? is played by a minimum of four players. One player is Mr. Wolf and stands at one end of the playing area, facing away from the other players, who stand at the opposite end. All players except Mr. Wolf chant in unison, "What time is it, Mr. Wolf?" and Mr. Wolf answers in one of two ways: Mr. Wolf may call a time (usually an hour ending in *o'clock*), or Mr. Wolf may call "Dinner time!" If Mr. Wolf answers with a time, the other players take that many steps toward Mr. Wolf. Then they ask the question again. If Mr. Wolf calls "Dinner time!" he is able to turn around and chase the other players back to their starting point, trying to tag them. If Mr. Wolf tags a player, that player becomes Mr. Wolf for the next round.

Animal Charades

Animal Charades needs at least four players, with all players sitting in a circle. One player acts out the movements and sounds of an animal for other players to guess. Players take turns guessing the animal chosen. The player who guesses correctly gets a turn to perform for the next round of play.

> **Variation:** To make the game more challenging, the player acting out the animal cannot make animal sounds as she is charading for other players.

Crabs on the Move

Crabs on the Move is played by a minimum of five players. One player is the leader, and all other players line up at one end of a marked playing area with their hands and feet on the floor and a small (unbreakable) object, such as a beanbag, balancing on their backs. At the leader's "Go" signal, players keep this position and race to the finish line on the other side of the playing area without bumping into each other and without the object falling off their back. If the object falls off of someone, that player must return to the starting line to begin again. The first player to cross the finish line with the object still on his back is the winner.

> **Variation:** All players move as a group toward the finish line without falling or losing their balance. If one player loses her object, everyone returns to the starting line to try again.

Giants in the Mirror

Giants in the Mirror needs at least two players, who stand facing each other. One player in each pair (or set of three if there is an odd number) is the giant and slowly acts out movements for the other player to copy. Players can make only movements that are big like giants, such as a giant brushing his teeth, a giant stretch, a giant smile, maybe even a giant laugh. The other player tries to copy the giant's movements or sounds as they are being done. Then players switch roles.

This Little Pig

This Little Pig is for two players. Each player is barefoot and seated facing the other. Both players do the same actions to the chant. Players wiggle their toes with their fingers, starting with their big toe and changing toes with each line of the chant:

This little piggy went to market. (Players wiggle the big toe.)

This little piggy stayed home. (Players wiggle the second toe.)

This little piggy had roast beef. (Players wiggle the middle toe.)

This little piggy had none. (Players wiggle the fourth toe.)

This little piggy said, "Wee, wee, wee, all the way home." (Players wiggle the last toe.)

Sweet Dreams

Sweet Dreams needs a minimum of three players. One player is the leader. All players except the leader start the game lying on the floor in a sleeping position. The leader says, "Sleeping, sleeping, everyone was sleeping. And when they woke up, they were all (sheep)." At this point, all players wake up and act out what the leader said. The leader can use the name of an animal, person, or object, such as a lion, football player, or zombie. At any time while players are acting out the character, the leader can say, "All (sheep) got tired and went back to sleep." At that time, players stop and pretend to sleep until the next round of play. The leader can change as often as the group decides.

Smile Trial

Smile Trial is played by a minimum of four players, who form a circle with one player in the middle. The player in the middle moves around the circle asking each player, "(Stephen), do you like me?" The player asked replies, "(Asker's name), I like you, but I just can't smile." If the player smiles or laughs as she replies, the two players switch roles. If she doesn't smile, the player can ask again, making funny faces or movements to get her to smile. If she still does not smile, the asker moves to another player in the circle and the game continues until someone smiles or laughs.

Name Train

Name Train needs at least four players. One player is the leader. All other players stand in a circle. The leader shuffles around the inside of the circle moving like a train and stops at any player saying, "Hi, my name is (Isabella)." The player stopped at replies, "Hi, (Isabella), my name is (Jade)." The leader raises one arm and motions to the player to get on the train. The other players chant "(Jade) . . . (Jade) . . . (Jade) . . . (Jade) . . . (Jade)." The second player holds onto the leader's waist, and the two players shuffle around the circle until the name train stops in front of another player in the circle. The game continues until all players are on the train.

Wiggles and Giggles

Wiggles and Giggles is played by a minimum of four players. One player is the leader. All players except the leader stand in a circle close enough to touch each other. The leader gives the players instructions, such as "Put your hand on the shoulder of a player next to you" or "Touch your chin with your hand." Players follow the leader's direction and cannot move until the leader gives the next command. If players move or giggle too much and lose their balance, they are out of the game. The last player to go down is the leader for the next round of play.

I Saw

 I Saw needs at least three players, and one player is the leader. All other players stand facing the same direction and are told by the leader to look carefully at everything around them in that area. Then the leader tells players to close their eyes and keep them shut. Players take turns telling each other something that they saw. Their answers must be different from the other players' answers given before them. Score can be kept to count how many items a player saw, or players can tally all of their answers together. When no player can add anything else to the I Saw list, a new leader takes over and instructs players to look in another direction for the next round of play.

> **Variations:** To make the game easier, players are told to look carefully at one player, then close their eyes and take turns telling something about that player, such as "She's wearing a pink shirt" or "His hair is brown." To make the game more challenging, after players have had time to look at things around them, the leader can remove one item while the players' eyes are closed. Then players open their eyes and guess what's been taken away.

I'm a Robot

I'm a Robot is played by a minimum of three players. One player is the leader. All other players stand spread out in a large playing area without touching each other. These players are the robots and are programmed to follow the beeping commands of the leader. Robots can walk only with straight legs and arms. Here are some examples of the leader's beeping commands:

One beep = robots walk straight ahead.

Two beeps = robots stop where they are.

Three beeps = robots turn around.

If the leader sees a robot who doesn't follow his command, that robot must sit down until the next round of play. The last standing robot becomes the new leader.

> Variation: Commands can be changed to make the game easier or additional ones added to make the game more challenging.

This Is the Way

This Is the Way is for any number of players. To start, players stand side by side without touching each other in an open playing area. Players chant the song here while they create their own actions to dramatize each verse.

This is the way the ladies ride,

Tre, tree, tre, tree, tre, tree, tre tree.

This is the way the ladies ride,

Tre, tree, tre, tree, tre, tree, tre tree.

This is the way the gentlemen ride,

Gallop-a-trot, gallop-a-trot.

This is the way the gentlemen ride,

Gallop-a-trot, gallop-a-trot.

This is the way the farmers ride,

Hobbley-hoy, hobbled-hoy.

This is the way the farmers ride,

Hobbley-hoy, hobbled-hoy.

Can You Do What I Do?

Can You Do What I Do? is played by a minimum of three players. One player is the leader. All other players stand spaced around the leader without touching each other. Players close

their eyes while the leader strikes a pose and says to the other players, "Can you do what I do?" Then players open their eyes and try to copy the leader's pose. After players have had time to copy the pose, they remain in that pose but close their eyes. Then the leader changes her pose and again tells the players, "Can you do what I do?" Players open their eyes and try to shift their position to match the leader's. The game ends when all players have had a turn to be the leader.

> Variations: To make the game more challenging, the leader makes a very subtle change, such as moving only a finger, changing his facial expression, or tilting his head in a different direction. Also, the leader might change his pose and add a motion such as raising his arm and waving.

What's Missing?

What's Missing? needs at least five players. One player is the guesser. All other players sit in a circle. The guesser sits in the middle of the circle and closes his eyes. While his eyes are closed, one player leaves the circle to hide in a place where she can't be seen. The guesser opens his eyes and guesses who is missing. Game rules are flexible so the guesser can have more than one guess. If he guesses correctly, the players switch places for another round of play. If not, the same player remains the guesser and the game begins again.

> Variations: After the missing player is hidden, other players switch places in the circle before the guesser opens his eyes. Another way to make the game more challenging is to have all players close their eyes while the guesser removes something he's wearing, such as a shoe, sock, or jacket. Then players open their eyes and guess what's missing.

The Changing Circle

The Changing Circle is played by a minimum of five players. One player is the leader. All other players hold hands and form a circle. After all players are in place, the leader gives directions on how the circle will look. For instance, the leader may say, "The circle is getting taller." At this point, players stand on tiptoe and hold that position until the leader gives another command, such as "The circle is shrinking" or "The circle is hopping." Players try to complete each order without letting go of the players' hands on either side of them. Players should be encouraged to look at each other and cooperate to follow the leader's directions. The game ends when all players have had a turn to be the leader.

CHAPTER 15

TRANSITION GAMES

 ### Improvise Spies

Improvise Spies is played by a minimum of two players. One player is the leader, and when she says, "I spy . . ." all other players ask, "What do you spy?" The leader replies, "I spy dancers dancing in place," or "I spy a rock band silently playing their instruments." At this point, the other players act out what the leader has spied until again she says "I spy." Then all players stop and ask, "What do you spy?" The game continues with the leader calling out other ideas such as, "I spy everyone making funny faces." The role of leader can be rotated through all players.

Flying High

This game needs at least three players. One player is the leader and names animals or objects that fly (or don't) to the other players. For example, the leader may say "Crows fly," "Bumblebees fly," "Helicopters fly," and "Beds fly." If the animal or object named is able to fly, players flap their arms and pretend to fly. If the object or animal does not fly, players cannot move their arms. The leader may try to trick other players by making a false statement or motions. If players imitate the leader by making an incorrect motion and are caught, they sit down until the next round of play. The last player standing has a turn to be the next leader.

> Variation: The leader calls different animals with appropriate sounds or actions, such as "Cats meow," "Hens cluck," "Horses trot," or "Ducks waddle," which must be imitated by other players.

Hot and Cold

Hot and Cold is played by a minimum of four players. One player is the guesser and leaves the group. The other players choose an object in the area the guesser will have to find when he returns. The guesser returns to the group and walks from place to place trying to locate the item the other players have chosen. Players help him find the object by humming or singing a familiar song and increasing the volume of their voices as he nears the object he is looking for and decreasing the volume of their chants when he moves away from it. The game ends when the object is finally found. Then another player assumes the role of the guesser and the game continues.

> Variation: Players say, "Warm," "Warmer," or "Hot" as the guesser gets closer and closer to the chosen object or "Cold," "Colder" or "Freezing" as she gets farther away from the object.

Simon Says "Got Ya"

Simon Says "Got Ya" needs a minimum of three players. This game is played like Simon Says (page 55), but Simon uses gestures that do not go with the directions he gives. Players must follow his directions (not his gestures) but only if he begins his commands with "Simon says." If Simon does not begin his commands this way, players do not obey. Any player who does so is out of the game. For instance, Simon may say, "Wiggle your nose" while he is wiggling his ear or "Simon says touch your toes" while he is touching his shoulders. If players follow Simon's gestures instead of his directions or follow the directions without the command "Simon Says," he says, "Simon got ya." Then the player sits down until the next round of play. The last player remaining becomes the next Simon.

Oh, Ah

Oh, Ah is played by at least four players and can be done while standing in a circle or waiting in a line. One player is the leader. If the players are in a line, the leader should be at the front. The game starts with all players holding hands. The leader squeezes the hand of the player on his right, and the player behind him continues the squeeze along the line or around the circle. When approximately half the players have been squeezed, the leader gives another squeeze to the player on his right and adds a sound such as "oh," with the players repeating the squeeze and the sound. When that has reached half the players, he adds another sound, such as "ah," "zoom," or "whee." The game is over when the last player finishes her sound. The role of leader can be rotated through all players.

All in One

All in One needs a minimum of six players. One player is the leader. All other players stand in a circle holding hands. The leader stands in the middle of the circle and calls one player at a time to join her in the middle while still holding the hands of other players. The goal is to see how many players will fit in the middle of the circle without players breaking their holds.

Body Language

Body Language is played by minimum of three players. One player is the leader and whispers a short sentence, such as "I like to ride my bike," "I'm tired," or "I'm dizzy" to another player. Then that player tries to act out exactly what the leader said while other players take turns guessing what the leader's sentence was. The first player to correctly guess the sentence becomes the leader for the next round. If players cannot guess the leader's sentence and give up, the leader remains the same for the next round of play.

I Got Your Back

I Got Your Back needs at least two players paired together. Players stand back-to-back with a partner with elbows locked and try to sit on the floor. When this is accomplished, the pair tries to stand up, pushing on each other's backs without using their hands. After the pair stands up, the players find another pair, and all four players stand back-to-back, hook elbows, and try to sit down and stand up together. The game can continue adding more pairs of players to the group until everyone is too exhausted to play any longer. Any extra player can be given the role of supervisor and assist players if needed to keep them from getting hurt.

Hop Till You Drop

Hop Till You Drop is played by a minimum of three players and is similar to Simon Says (page 55). One player is the leader and gives other players hopping directions using the names of animals, such as "Kangaroo says," "Froggie says," or "Mr. Rabbit says." If the leader gives a direction to players without mentioning the animal's name first and the players hop, they are out of the game until the next round of play. Some hopping directions can include:

- Hop on both feet, only your right foot, or only your left foot.
- Hop with another player.
- Hop around in a circle.
- Hop backward without touching another player.
- Hop toward another player and stop in front of him.
- Hop in place.

The last player to remain standing is the winner and the new leader for the next round of play.

Rock, Paper, Scissors

Rock, Paper, Scissors is for two players. Following are the hand motions for this game:

- Rock is a fist.
- Paper is a flat hand.
- Scissors are the pointer and middle fingers extended, making a V configuration.

Two players sit or stand face to face. In unison, players tap one fist in the palm on their other hand two times and on the third time, show their chosen motion, either rock, paper, or scissors. Winning hands are any of the following: Rock breaks scissors. Scissors cuts paper. Paper covers rock. A point is given to the player with a winning hand. If both players have identical motions, no points are awarded. The first player to get to a predetermined number of points is the winner.

Guess Who?

Guess Who? is played by a minimum of four players.

One player is the leader. This game is similar to Twenty Questions (page 50). The object is to guess the identity of a player the leader secretly chooses. After the leader chooses a player, other players take turns asking the leader only yes and no questions, such as "Is the player a girl?" "Does she have green eyes?" and so on until twenty questions have been asked. The player who correctly identifies the chosen player becomes the next leader. If the player is not guessed, the leader remains the same for the next round of play.

My Happy Place

My Happy Place needs a minimum of two players and challenges players to think about what makes them happy. When players think of something that makes them happy, they take turns acting out their happiness, such as "I'm happy when I'm eating pizza" or "Hugging my dog makes me happy." Instead, players may choose to talk about what makes them happy or need some suggestions to get them thinking. The following list may be helpful in getting the game started:

- What one thing (person, food, animal, or game) makes you happy?
- What is something that just happened to you that made you happy?
- Did someone do something to make you happy?

Players take turns guessing what actions each player is acting out. The player who makes a correct guess gets to be the actor for the next round of play.

Read My Mind

Read My Mind is a group game played by a minimum of five players. Two players take the roles of the mind reader and her assistant. They try to prove to the other players they can read each other's mind. The trick is that the correct object will be the first one after a black object or other agreed-upon colored object. To begin, the mind reader leaves the playing area while the other players and the assistant choose a visible object. Then the mind reader returns to the group. The assistant asks the mind reader questions to see if he knows what the chosen object is. For example, the assistant can ask, "Is it the red rug?" or "Is it the black sofa?" The mind reader replies no to both. But when the assistant says, "Is it the white pillow?" the mind reader replies yes, as the pillow is the object mentioned after the black sofa. The game ends when a player figures out the trick and shares this with other players. Unfortunately, this game cannot be played again after all players know the mind reader's trick.

Who Can?

Who Can? needs at least two players. Players take turns asking each other to do silly things:

- Wink with one eye or both eyes.
- Roll your tongue.
- Wiggle your ears or wiggle your nose.
- Snap your fingers on both hands or one hand.
- Touch your ear with your elbow.
- Whistle.
- Twiddle your thumbs.
- Rub your stomach and pat your head at the same time.
- Make a popping sound with your tongue on the roof of your mouth.

The game continues until all players are too silly to continue (or are rolling on the floor with laughter).

What Am I Counting?

What Am I Counting? is played by a minimum of three players. One player is the counter, who stands in front of the other players and chooses an object in the playing area to secretly count. Without pointing to any objects or making any gestures, he begins counting out loud, starting with one. The other players take turns trying to guess what he is counting, such as windows, books, or chairs. The objects being counted have to be visible to all players. The player who guesses the object correctly gets the next turn to be the counter.

> Variation: The counter selects a type of object, such as tables, chairs, or objects of a certain color, secretly counts the number of the selected objects, and challenges players to count as many as they can find within a predetermined amount of time. The winner is the first player to get the answer correct.

Stone-Faced

Stone-Faced is for two players, who sit or stand face to face with eyes closed. Together, they count "1, 2, 3," open their eyes and look into their opponent's eyes. Players cannot laugh, poke each other, nod, nor blink, and whoever flinches, smiles, or laughs first is out, with the stone-faced player the winner.

Magic

Magic needs a minimum of three players sitting in chairs. One player is the leader and holds two sticks. The leader either crosses the two sticks or holds each stick upright, one in each hand. Then she says either "These sticks are crossed" or "These sticks are uncrossed," regardless of the position of the sticks. For instance, she may cross the sticks but say, "These sticks are uncrossed." The leader passes the sticks to the player on her right who tries to figure out how to hold them and repeats the sentence made by the leader. The trick is the leader says the sticks are crossed if her legs are crossed and if they aren't crossed, neither are the sticks in the sentence. The leader either agrees or disagrees with the player's sentence. If the player is incorrect, he passes the sticks to the next player for her turn. The first player to figure out that the sentence refers to legs and not sticks and answer correctly is the winner.

> Variation: A player who knows the answer whispers it to the leader and play continues while other players try to figure out the trick or everyone else gives up.

Bubbles

Bubbles is played by at least two players. Players pretend to blow a bubble of any size around themselves to create their own bubble space. To define their bubble space, players can extend their arms straight in front of them, out to their sides, or make a circle by joining their hands in front of them. Players must move very slowly and carefully so their bubbles don't pop or they don't get too close to other players' bubbles. If two players collide, their bubbles burst, and they are out of the game. The winner is the last player with her bubble intact.

> Variations: Two players work together in any way they want to form a bubble and then move together without hitting another bubble pair or popping their bubble. In another version, all players join hands to form a giant bubble and then try to move it from place to place, make it float in the air, or dance on the floor.

Lights, Camera, Action!

Lights, Camera, Action! needs at least two players. One player is the photographer. While the other players watch him, the photographer pretends to snap a photo of any object or person visible to all other players with his magic, invisible camera but does not tell anyone what he has taken a photo of. Then he gives a clue about what the photo includes, such as "A person with black hair" or "Something blue on the bookshelf." Players take turns guessing what the photo is. If no player guesses correctly, the photographer gives another clue, and players take turns guessing again. The player who gives the right answer first becomes the next photographer.

Silence Is Golden

Silence Is Golden is played by a minimum of four players. Players cannot speak to each other during this game but can communicate with gestures or any other nonverbal way. One player, the leader, can speak. The leader gives players a task, and when she says "Go," they try to accomplish the task, without talking, before time runs out. For example, the leader may ask the group to form a line by their height or according to their birthdates by the time she counts to fifty.

CHAPTER 16

TRAVEL GAMES

> Though everyone traveling is welcome to join in these fun games, it is suggested that drivers either have minimal involvement in the game or not participate to keep their focus and attention on driving safely.

 ### Corn, Corn, Corn, Corn

Before Corn, Corn, Corn, Corn begins, each player chooses something seen often from the vehicle's windows, such as corn and cows on the prairies or palm trees and surfboards in beach areas. Players write or draw a picture of each item on a piece of paper. Every time one of the items is seen, they mark a tally on their paper. Players compare scores and what they saw at the end of the trip or periodically during travel such as from one stop to the next or at the end the day.

 ### First Letters

Players write the first letter of their names on a piece of paper and watch for these letters on license plates of passing vehicles. Whenever the letter appears, a point is scored. The first player to have all letters in his name appear five (or ten) times wins the game.

 ### How Many Routes?

In How Many Routes?, before the trip begins, the driver circles two cities, lakes, rivers, or points of interest on a map or printout that will be used only for this game. Then players take turns finding a route to travel between these locations. Players trace their route and identify it as theirs either by using different colored highlight pens or writing their names next to the route they've marked on the map. This game helps all players learn to read a map by seeing if the driver is following their suggested route.

Population

One player is the leader of Population and chooses a town or city from a map. She shows this location to the other players without showing the population information on the map. Players take turns guessing how many people live in that town or city. The player with the closest guess wins and gets to be the next leader.

Animal, Plant, or Not Alive?

In Animal, Plant, or Not Alive? one player is the leader and thinks of something familiar to everyone else and then tells others if it is an animal, plant, or not alive. Because the "not alive" category is so broad, it is best to narrow the chosen item by limiting it to things seen in the immediate surroundings. Each player takes a turn asking the leader about the chosen object with a question that requires a yes or no answer and then takes a guess of what this could be. The player who makes the correct guess selects the next object.

Sightseer

One player, the leader, chooses a category, such as the color of the next car, the type of animal next seen, or the name of the next fast-food restaurant. Other players take turns trying to guess what will be seen next. The player who guesses correctly scores a point. This game is played up to a predetermined number of points. The first player to reach that number of points is the winner and is the next leader to choose a category.

Numbers on a Plate

Numbers on a Plate is played in a bus or car. Players take turns looking at passing vehicles' license plates and collecting the numbers that they see on those tags. Player one gets the first vehicle, player two, the second, and so on. The goal is to be the first player to collect all numbers from one to twelve in numerical order. The numbers can appear anywhere on the license plate. For instance, 8410 counts for one, while 2074 counts for two. However, the numerals ten, eleven, and twelve must be together, so 9105 counts as ten, while 4811 counts for eleven. The first player to collect all twelve numbers is the winner.

> Variations: Players try to spot license plates with the smallest number, highest number, most repeated numbers, or most numbers in numerical order. When a player sees a plate that beats the last one seen, she scores a point. If another player spots a plate that beats that one, he gets the point and the last player's previous point is canceled out. At the end of the trip, players total their points and the highest total is the winner. In another version, one player goes first and spots a license plate with at least three letters. The player tells the other players what three letters she has spotted, and they take turns trying to make up a sentence starting words using all letters anywhere in the sentence from the license plate. For instance, if the letters *l*, *m*, *d* are spotted, a player making the sentence "<u>L</u>et's <u>m</u>ake a <u>d</u>eal" scores a point. The player with the most points after a predetermined amount of time is the winner.

Ten States

Players take turns looking at the license plates on vehicles that pass them. For instance, player one looks at the first vehicle, and player two looks at the second vehicle. As they see the license plate of the vehicle, players write down the state where the license was issued. The first player to record license plates from ten different states is the winner.

Roadside Animals

Roadside Animals is a team game played by a minimum of two players. One team or player looks out the windows of one side of the vehicle, and the other team gets the other side. The goal is for each team to see and count as many roadside animals as possible from their windows. Each team counts only the animals on their side of the road. Any animal (including birds, fish, insects, reptiles, and mammals) counts as one point. Not more than one animal of each kind can be counted in a single herd. The first team to reach a predetermined number of points is the winner.

> Variation: A twist on this game is The Wildlife Game in which animals more difficult to spot get more points. Geese and ducks get five points, while a deer and pheasant get fifty points. Whoever calls the animals first gets the points, and each member of a herd of deer gets counted.

 ## License Plates

License Plates is to be played while on the road and is best played when a variety of license plates can be seen. Each player chooses a different destination on a map. After all players have chosen their destination, they look at the license plates of passing vehicles and try to find ones from five states that can take them to their chosen destination. For instance, a player may choose New York City as her destination. To win, she must find vehicles from five different states that can get her to New York City from the location of the vehicle before any other player does. Players can get there by roundabout routes, but the first player to reach his location wins.

> Note: Having a road atlas or map can help players find routes as well as settle any disagreements about navigating to destinations.

 ## Are We There Yet?

All players agree on a destination or point on their journey without knowing how many miles away this is. Each player guesses how much time it will take to get there. When players arrive at the destination, the guesses are compared with the actual arrival time. The player with the closest guess wins. The winner chooses the new destination for the next round of play.

Alphabet Race

Alphabet Race is a team game played by a minimum of two players. One team or player looks out the windows of one side of the vehicle and the other player or team gets the other side. The object of the game is to spot all letters of the alphabet in order. Letters on road signs, store signs or windows, billboards, and words on the sides of vehicles all count. Each team counts only the letters on its side of the road. As soon as *A* is seen, the player points to it and calls it out, then goes to *B*. The winning player or team is the one that reaches *Z* first.

Color Collecting

One player chooses a color, and other players look out the windows for vehicles of the chosen color and call out the color immediately after spotting one. The first player to call out scores a point. When two or more players call out together, nobody scores. After a car is found, the next player chooses a color and play continues. The first player to score a predetermined number of points wins the game.

Alphabet Trip

The first player of Alphabet Trip begins with the letter *A* and names a destination starting with this letter, such as "I'm going to Alaska (or Albuquerque or Austria)." The next player says, "What will you do when you get there?" The initial letter of each word in the first player's reply must also begin with *A* so she may say, "Act awful" or "Ask Aunt Ann for apples." Then it's the second player's turn, and he must name a destination beginning with the letter *B*, such as "I'm going to Brooklyn." When asked what he might do, the reply may be, "Buy birdseed." The game continues as long as there's interest or until all letters have been used.

What Did I See?

What Did I See? is an "on the way back home" game. One player gives clues about a place, thing, activity, person, or event experienced on the trip without naming it. Other players guess what this is, from the clues given. The player to guess the correct answer first is the winner and gets the next turn to give clues on what was seen or done during the trip.

I'm Thinking Of

I'm Thinking Of is played by a minimum of two players. One player is the leader, who chooses an object in the car or bus and keeps it a secret. When the item is chosen, she says, "I'm thinking of something in the car and . . ." then gives a hint as to the object's location, color, or size. Other players take turns guessing what the object is. The first player to guess correctly is the winner and the leader for the next round of play.

I Took a Trip

The object of this game is to remember a sequence. One player begins with "I took a trip, and in my suitcase I put . . ." which can be anything from a toothbrush or a pair of socks to something unusual such as a baseball bat, Silly Putty, or even a hamburger. The next player repeats the sentence of the first player and adds another item to the suitcase. Play continues with each player repeating the items of the previous players and adding their own item to the suitcase. As the list gets longer, players who forget the exact order of items are out until the next round. When only one player remains, that player is the winner.

Road Sign Quiz

One player is the leader, who selects a specific road sign for each round of play, such as a pedestrian crosswalk sign, railroad sign, or detour sign. All players look for this sign, and the first to find it scores a point. For young players who are not familiar with the signs, the leader points to the chosen sign either along the road (or on a map) and asks players to find another sign identical to that one. Signs seen frequently, such a speed limit signs, highway mile marker signs, and exit signs can keep players more interested (and successful) in playing the game. The first player to find the sign is the leader for the next round of play.

Ten Pairs

Each player chooses a number from zero to nine before the game begins. Then players watch for pairs of their number to appear on license plates of passing vehicles. Two of a given number found anywhere on the plate count as a pair. Three of the number count for two pair, and four of the number count as three pairs. The first player to reach ten pairs is the winner.

Night Lights

Night Lights is played after the sun goes down. The object of the game is to be the first player (or team) to call out ten blinker lights from other vehicles. Players are divided into two teams; one team (or player) looks for vehicles with their right blinker lights on, while the others look for left blinker lights. When a lit blinker is found, players call out either "left" or "right." If a player or team calls out the wrong signal, the opposing player or team automatically scores an extra point. The first person or team to reach ten points wins the game.

A Mile to Win

One player is the leader and chooses a letter. Other players try to spot as many objects as they can from their window beginning with that letter. For instance, if the letter *F* is chosen, players may find a farm, fence, field, fountain, and so on. A site may be counted by only one player (the first to locate it). If an object is called out by two players at the same time, each player receives a point. The first player to score the most points after traveling for exactly one mile wins the round and gets to choose the beginning letter for the next round.

The Wave Game

The object is to get the most points by waving to people passing by and getting them to wave back. Each player gets five minutes to wave to people outside of the vehicle. If they wave back, the player gets a point for each person returning his wave. When all players have had a turn, the player with the most points is declared the "waver winner" and gets waves from everyone inside the car.

> Variation: To make the game more interesting, point values can be assigned according to the colors of the wavers' vehicle. For example, orange or yellow vehicles are worth ten points, green are worth five points, red are worth two points, and all other colors are worth only one point.

Fifty States

In Fifty States, one player volunteers or is the leader and gives the "Go" signal. Then all players have three minutes to write down as many of the fifty states as they can. Two-letter abbreviations may be used to represent the states; for example, *KS* for *Kansas* or *AL* for *Alabama*. Younger players can whisper their states to an older player who writes them. Answers can be shared to see if all fifty states were identified by the group, or individual players can receive one point for each state identified. In a competitive round, the player with the most points wins.

Odd and Even Tags

Odd and Even Tags is a bus or car travel game. Players choose either odd or even numbers prior to the start of the game. One player is the leader. At the leader's "Go" signal, players begin watching for license plates of passing vehicles. The odd player (or team) gets one point for each license plate that ends with an odd number, while the even player (or team) receives a point for all plates that end with an even number. Zero is considered an even number. The first player or team to reach a predetermined number of points, such as twenty-five, wins the game.

Inching Along

Inching Along is played in a bus or car. At the beginning of the day's travel, players are shown the route for the trip on a map or printout and the distance to be covered by the driver. Players choose a place along the way on the map and circle their spot with their name or initials. After all players have had an opportunity to mark the map, players watch for the places they circled. When each point on the trip is reached, a line is drawn through the circled location, the next destination is announced, and the search for the new place continues until at long last, the final destination is reached.

Travel Hunt

Travel Hunt, a scavenger hunt, is played in a bus or car. Players are divided into teams, or each player plays independently if there are few players. Players have a list of items to search for on the trip (for players with limited or no reading skills, a list with small pictures of the items will help them be successful). Only one team or player can claim each item. After an item has been found, that item is crossed off the list and marked with the initials of the spotting team or player. A point is awarded to the team or player finding each item. Points are tallied after all items on the list have been found. Winners are the ones with the most points. Here are some suggested items to seach for:

- license plate with the letter Z on it
- RV or camping trailer
- three birds flying together
- water tower
- plane
- bridge
- school bus
- law enforcement vehicle
- boat on a trailer
- motorcycle
- detour sign

- billboard with no numbers on it
- spotted horse
- sign with a flashing light
- bird's nest

Pick a Car, Any Car

Pick a Car, Any Car is a bus or car game. One player is the leader and chooses a type of vehicle that is often seen on the road, for instance, a convertible, moving van, double-cab truck, or four-door car. Each player guesses how many of the selected type vehicle will be seen en route to the destination, or if traveling a long distance, a location along the way or a set period of time. Players write down or announce their guess before the game begins. The winner is the player with the closest guess to the actual number of vehicles spotted during the playing time. Then it's the winner's turn to choose the type of vehicle for the next round of play.

The Map Game

The Map Game needs a map or printout of the fifty states. When players see a license plate from a state, they circle or highlight the name of that state and add their initials to the map. The game ends when plates from all states have been found. The winner is the player who found the most license plates.

> Variation: Finding only the lower forty-eight states may make the game easier and faster. Five bonus points can be given for Alaska or Hawaii (unless traveling there!) or government license plates.

Scenic Games

It's the goal of this game to find items that begin with the first six letters in a player's name. Players write the first six letters of their name across the top of a sheet of paper. If a player's name has fewer than six letters, she adds enough letters of her middle or last name to get to six letters. Players get fifteen minutes to write down (or draw) objects on their sheet of paper that they find in the surroundings (inside or outside of the vehicle) or in passing vehicles that begin with the same letter as the six letters on their page. The winner is the player with the most items listed on his sheet at the end of the fifteen minutes.

Add an Action

One player is the leader of Add an Action and starts with a simple action, such as clapping his hands twice. The next player copies that action and adds an action of her own. Then the third player copies the first two actions and adds one of his own. Each player continues to take a turn with the sequencing of actions getting longer and more difficult to follow. A player who misses an action is out and must wait for the next game to begin. The winner is the last player to remember the entire sequence of actions.

> **Note: It is suggested the driver give permission for this game in advance and always reserves the right for it to be stopped at any time if the noise or excitement is distracting.**

Map Spotters

In the Map Spotters game, one player is the leader, who locates a place on a map and tells only the name of the location to other players. Then players are given the map and take turns trying to find this place within a designated time limit. Players with limited map-reading skills should be given a longer amount of time. If the location is found within the time limit, the finder scores one point and chooses the next map spot. If no player finds the chosen location, the leader names another place to find on the map, and play resumes. The winner is the player with the highest score when interest wanes or when a preset total score has been reached.

Blind Guessing

One player is the leader and selects an object a mile or less down the road (within sight of everyone), such as a gas station, water tower, or billboard, and points it out to the other players. All players close their eyes tightly and shout "Now" when they think the vehicle they are in is passing the object. To avoid accusations of cheating, it is a good idea for players to lean forward with their heads on their knees. As soon as a player has shouted "Now," she sits up, and the leader checks her accuracy without making any comment about her guess until other players have had their turn to guess. The winner is the player whose guess is closest to the location.

 ## Counting Up

All players look for numbers on signs outside the vehicle, such as on billboards, road signs, or signs on buildings. Players concentrate only on numbers ending in a five or zero, such as five or twenty. Only the first player who sees a number may count it; the first player to reach one hundred wins.

> Variations: The game can be changed so players look only for even numbers. The winner is the player who reaches fifty first. In another version, players can look for only odd numbers or multiples of any number from one through nine.

CHAPTER 17

WORD GAMES

Ghost

Ghost is played by a minimum of three players with spelling skills. The first player starts the game by saying a letter. Then other players take turns adding a letter to the previous player's letter while still being able to spell an actual word. If the next player does not believe the word chain is creating an actual word, he may challenge the previous player to prove she is spelling a word. For example, if the first letter is *P* and the next player adds a *D*, a player can say, "I challenge," because there are no words that begin that way. If the challenged player can spell a word correctly, he wins the game.

The player who ends the word by adding the last letter, and no other player can add another letter onto it, loses the round of play. For instance if the word chain is "f-a-i-r" and the next player adds "y" on the end of the word because she's finished "Fairy," she loses that round. Each time a player loses a round, he earns a letter *G*, *H*, *O*, *S*, or *T*. The first player to get letters to spell *GHOST* is out of the game.

Password

Password needs at least four players with spelling skills. Players are divided into two teams of similar ability if possible. Before the game begins, each player writes between five to ten words on small pieces of paper (one word per piece of paper), folds them and puts them in a pile with the words of their teammates. These words become the passwords. A player from each team is the leader for a round of play and stands in front of her team. Both teams pull a piece of paper from their opposing team's password pile and share it among themselves without letting the leader know the word. Then team players take turns giving a one-word clue to their leader to help her guess the password. The leader to guess the password first gets one point. The first team to score ten points wins.

Two Truths and a Lie

Two Truths and a Lie is played by a minimum of two players. Players take turns saying two facts and one lie about themselves. The opposing player can accept each statement as true or say, "I doubt it" if he thinks the statement is a lie. If a player is able to identify his opponent's lie, he gets one point for identifying it. However, if the statement is true, he loses a point from his total point count. The first player to get five points wins.

Number, Please

Number, Please needs at least two players. One player secretly picks a number from one to ten. Then she tells a story using her chosen number in each sentence along with any other number from one to ten. The chosen number must be in all sentences, while the other numbers vary from sentence to sentence. For instance, the storyteller might say, "Long ago there lived five fairies in a tree four feet high. The five fairies had two pet goats and six chickens to take care of. The eight pets got up every morning at five o'clock." The story continues until a player guesses that five was her chosen number. Then it's his turn to be the storyteller.

What a Story!

What a Story! is played by a minimum of two players. Players give ideas for story genres, such as a science fiction story, funny story, adventure story, or an animal or nature story. Then each player says the name of a person, animal, place, or thing to include in the story, such as *airplane*, *pizza*, *kangaroo*, or *New York City*. At least five or six words are needed to write a story. Players are given a short time (ten or less minutes) to think of a story, and if preferred, write it on a piece of paper using as many of the chosen words as they can that were mentioned. Each player has a turn to read or tell her story to the group. No winners or losers in this game, just a lot of creative fun.

Double the Fun

Double the Fun needs at least two players. One player is the leader. The leader starts the game with a two-part word, such as *time out* or *Silly Putty*, or a compound word, such as *butterfly*, *windmill*, or *moonbeam*. The next player says a word that begins with the second part of the previous player's word. For instance, if the leader says "time out," the first player can say "out loud," the second player may say "loud sound," and the third player can say "sound off." The game continues until all players are out of words to continue the chain. A new leader is chosen and starts another round of play with new double or compound words.

Name That Critter

Name That Critter is played by a minimum of three players, who take turns giving short descriptions of animals, either real or imaginary. The first player gives a description of an animal to the other players. For example, "Name the critter who builds dams by chewing trees that fall across streams" (a beaver). "Name the critter that is a large, long-legged purple bird with polka-dot feathers on its wings" (an imaginary bird that could be called a "Purple Polka-Dotter" or a "Purple Polka-Dotted Winger"). Players take turns guessing the animal being described. The first player to name the animal scores a point. The decision of the best name for imaginary animals is made by the player who described the animal. After an animal has been guessed, another player has a turn to describe his animal for the other players. The winner is the first player to get five points.

I Was So Hungry I Ate . . .

I Was So Hungry I Ate . . . needs at least two players. One player is the leader. The leader starts the game by secretly choosing a food and identifying it by the letter that it starts with. She says, "I was so hungry I ate something that starts with (*C*)." Players take turns guessing what she could have eaten, such as "cracker," "chocolate," "cookies." The player who guesses the right answer is the new leader and starts the next round of play.

Variations: One player chooses a letter for the game, and players take turns telling what they ate that starts with the chosen letter. Play continues until no player can think of an appropriate word to add. The last player to think of a word scores a point. For a more challenging game, players think of a food that begins with the final letter of the previous player's food. For instance, if the previous player's word was "cookies," the next player must give a food that starts with "s," such as "spaghetti." In another version, the category of foods is narrowed to certain types of foods, such as only vegetables, fruits, desserts, or beverages.

Who Am I?

Who Am I? is played by a minimum of four players. One player is the mystery person and leaves the playing area or covers his eyes and ears. Meanwhile, the other players choose a new identity for him, someone he knows or has heard of. When the players have made their decision, the mystery person returns or uncovers his eyes and ears and asks questions to guess who he is. The only questions he can ask are ones with "yes," "no," or "don't know" answers. The mystery person can either ask as many questions as he wants during a predetermined amount of time, or the game can be played in the Twenty Questions (page 50) format, limiting his questions to twenty. After he is done asking questions, the mystery person has three chances to guess who he is. He scores three points if he is right on the first try, two if his second guess is right, and one for the right answer on his third try. If he cannot guess by his third try, the other players tell him his identity, and a new mystery person is chosen for the next round of play.

Initial This

Initial This needs at least three players. They score one point for identifying any animal, person, place, or object that starts with the same letter as their first name. Players take turns giving their words, while one player tallies the players' correct answers. Play continues until players cannot add another word beginning with the first letter in their name. During the second round of play, points are given for words that start with the same letter as a player's last name. To extend the game, players' middle initials can be used for additional points. The winner is the player with the most points after all rounds of play.

Orderly Words

Orderly Words is played by a minimum of two players. One player chooses any word and calls it out to the other players. The next player gives a word that is somehow connected with the word chosen by the first player. Fox example if the first word was "apple," the second player could say "pie." The third player chooses a word that is connected to the last word mentioned, such as "slice." Players keep taking turns and adding words until someone is stuck and can't think of a related word. The winner is the last player to add a word to the word chain. Then she is the new leader and gets to start another round of play with the word of her choice.

You Don't Say

You Don't Say needs at least two players, who together decide on a word that no one can say, such as "I" or "you," in a predetermined amount of time. Then players try to trick each other into saying the selected word while they are talking. It is best to have a scorekeeper, but players can keep track of their own points on a sheet of paper. Every time players speak the forbidden word, a point is added to the player's list. The winner is the player with the least amount of points at the end of the time limit.

Word Lightning

Word Lightning is played by a minimum of four players. One player is the leader. During each turn, the leader gives a player a letter, and the player has one minute each to think of as many words that start with that letter as possible. The leader keeps count of each player's total. When all players have been given a turn, the player with the highest word count is the winner.

Who Likes It?

Who Likes It? needs at least three players. One player is the leader and names a kind of food eaten by animals, such as hay, bananas, peanuts, or nuts. Then players take turns giving the names of animals that eat that food, and the leader keeps a tally of each player's answers. For example, if "nuts" was the chosen food, correct answers could include squirrels, chipmunks, mice, or raccoons. The player with the most correct answers in each round becomes the leader for the next round of play.

My Neighbor's Cat

My Neighbor's Cat is played by a minimum of two players. One player is the leader. The leader starts the game by picking a letter of the alphabet, telling it to the other players, and using it at least twice to describe a cat. For example, if the leader chose A, he could say, "My neighbor's cat is an amazing cat, and her name is Abby." The next player must use two different words starting with A to describe the cat, such as "My neighbor's cat is adventurous and always active." After all players have had a turn, another round of play starts with a different letter to describe a cat. Play continues until everyone agrees to quit and play another game.

When, Why, Where

When, Why, Where needs at least two players. One player is the leader. The leader thinks of a secret object that other players take turns trying to identify by asking questions that start with "When . . . ," "Why . . . ," or "Where . . ." The leader must answer all questions honestly but tries to keep the object a secret as long as possible. For example, if the object she chose is a "car," this might be the question-response:

Question: "When do you use it?" Answer: "Every day."

Question: "Why do you have it?" Answer: "To help me shop."

Question: "Where do you use it?" Answer: "Outside."

The first player to guess the secret object becomes the new leader and starts the next round of play.

My Dad Owns a Store

My Dad Owns a Store is played by a minimum of three players. One player is selected to be the writer and begins the game saying, "My dad owns a store, and in it, he sells things that begin with (B)." Players take turns adding items typically bought in a store, such as bread, a broom, and bubble gum. Play continues until all players are out of B words. The next writer is the player who added the last word to the list. Then he continues the game with a new letter. The game can continue as long as there is interest from players.

Variation: The game can be made more challenging by choosing a particular kind of store such as a toy store, sporting goods store, or grocery store, and objects must be sold in the store type chosen to make the list.

APPENDIX A

RAINY DAY GAMES

Fantastic Games to Play When the Weather Outside Isn't So Fantastic

- Set up indoor floor games such as hopscotch or circle beanbag toss, using masking tape.
- Put on music and have a karaoke concert.
- Have an indoor sporting event with contests, such as toss the hot pad or oven mitt into a pan, sock ball soccer, or broom and jar lid curling.
- Put food coloring and dishwashing liquid in a container. Wash all the dirty toys.
- Bring out a box of toothpicks and play Pick-Up Sticks.
- Create a touchy-feely box, and fill it with mystery things to guess.
- Build a blanket or beach towel tent. Use only flashlights, and tell stories inside it.
- Play the game Islands (page xx) using pillows.
- Make your own Twister game on a tiled floor, using one color, letter, or word per tile.
- Play the staring game with a flashlight on your face.
- Bring out a deck of cards. Make up your own game.
- Invent your own language.
- Set up an indoor basketball game using an empty wastepaper basket and rolled up socks.
- Take a broom, play some music, and limbo.
- Hang spoons off your nose, chin, and cheeks.

- Make a paper donkey and play Pin the Tail on the Donkey.
- Make up your own dance routine while humming a song you made up.
- Place a large ball between your legs and see how far you can walk without dropping it.
- Set up a stage and have your own air band concert.
- Fill an empty spray bottle (set on "stream") with colored water and make spray paintings on paper towels or paper coffee filters.
- Set up an indoor obstacle course.
- Draw silly portraits of each other.
- Build a city out of boxes.
- Bring out a box of buttons and invent a game (for players three and older)
- Make paper airplanes and fly them.
- Find words nobody knows, and write your own definitions.
- Have a pillowcase race.

Smile and laugh often. The weather outside will change soon.

APPENDIX B

INDEX OF GAMES BY TITLE